CASTRO'S REVOLUTION

Myths and Realities

CASTRO'S REVOLUTION

Myths and Realities

THEODORE DRAPER

FREDERICK A. PRAEGER, *Publishers*
New York • Washington

BOOKS THAT MATTER

Published in the United States of America in 1962 by
Frederick A. Praeger, Inc., Publishers
111 Fourth Avenue, New York, N.Y. 10003

Eighth Printing, 1967

Library of Congress Catalog Card Number: 62-13305

Printed in the United States of America

FOREWORD

The circumstances behind the three essays in this book in part determined their form and content. They were written independently at intervals of about six months in response to the pressure of events. The first originated as a critical review of books on Cuba under Castro that appeared toward the end of 1960. As I worked on this review, I became dissatisfied with criticism only, and I felt the need to indicate what I considered to be more valid answers to some of the questions raised. Thus the article came to be half criticism, half reconstruction. The second was called forth by the ill-fated invasion of Cuba in April, 1961. Yet I did not limit myself to the invasion, and I made some effort to deal with what seemed to me to be the larger forces at work. The third was undertaken at the end of 1961 with the official transformation of Cuba into a "Marxist-Leninist" state on the Soviet model, and here I sought to trace the course of Fidel Castro's open avowal of his conversion to the Communist ideology and Party organization.

I was, in effect, primarily interested in searching for the nature and direction of Castro's regime at a time when these were still highly confused and controversial issues.

Although these three lengthy articles were written independently, the very events that brought them forth caused them to be closely interrelated. One leads into the other, in the same way that the Cuban story itself unfolded. To some extent, they represent a continuing struggle on my part to understand the Cuban reality. Wherever the flow of thought in each article seemed to require another reference to a previously mentioned point, I have permitted the original version to stand, even at the risk of some repetition. I have revised and enlarged these articles, but I have seen no reason to make any essential changes in interpretation or viewpoint. However, some important material, such as the evidence from Cuban Communist sources on the origin of official Castro-Communist collaboration on pp. 53–56 and the more extended discussion of United States policy on pp. 160–64, is new.

The first two sections were originally published in *Encounter* and as special supplements of *The New Leader*. The third section was issued in pamphlet form by *Encounter*. All three appeared in Spanish in *Cuadernos*, published in Paris.

I have added a letter to the *New Left Review*, published in London, as an Appendix because it may clarify some matters, both major and minor. The inclusion of the exchange of letters between Herbert Matthews and myself will, I believe, serve the same purpose. This entire work was made possible through the support of the Congress for Cultural Freedom, and I am particularly indebted to Michael Josselson and Melvin J. Lasky for their encouragement and long-suffering cooperation. I am, of course, solely responsible for the views expressed in these pages.

CONTENTS

CASTRO'S REVOLUTION

Myths and Realities

I. THE TWO REVOLUTIONS

Who is Fidel Castro? What is he? In the first months of his regime, Castro used to speak of "humanism," which he defined as "liberty with bread without terror" —hardly a political or social program. But after trying it out a few times, he dropped it in favor of even more ambiguous formulas. When he or his associates were asked what kind of society they were building or what it should be called, they usually answered that they were building "a reality, not a theory," or that they were interested "in deeds, not words," or that their revolution was "indigenously Cuban."

At a youth congress in Havana in August, 1960, however, Ernesto Guevara, Minister of Industries and former President of the National Bank of Cuba—who signed its banknotes with his nickname, "Che," nothing more —took a long step toward giving the regime an ideology and a name. Since Guevara was then the ideological mentor of Castro's regime, he had the habit of saying one day what Castro would say weeks or months later. He said: "What is our ideology? If I were asked whether our revolution is Communist, I would define it as Marxist. Our revolution has discovered by its methods the paths that Marx pointed out." In "Notes for the Study of the Ideology of the Cuban Revolution," published in October, 1960, in the magazine *Verde Olivo*, the official organ of the Cuban armed forces, Guevara wrote: "The principal actors of this revolution had no coherent theoretical criteria; but it cannot be said that they were ignorant of the various concepts of history, society, economics, and revolution which are being discussed in the world today." Then he declared: "We, practical revolutionaries, initiating our own struggle, simply fulfill laws foreseen by Marx the scientist."

These statements were far less revealing and straightforward than they seemed. Did Guevara mean to imply that the ideology was "Marxist" but not "Communist"? Was it the "Marxism" of the Communists or some other "Marxism"? Did Fidel, Guevara, and the others really come upon Marxism as if they were bright but naïve children rediscovering the roundness of the earth? Could the "laws" of "Marx the scientist," which have not been fulfilled anywhere else, be fulfilled in the little island of Cuba by those who did not know what they were doing until after they had done it?

Guevara's explanation obviously explained too little or too much. But Castro, Guevara, and other Cuban leaders spoke much more freely and at far greater length to a chosen few who became their foreign interpreters and apologists. This growing band, however, did not have an easy time of it and was for a while forced to do much of the theorizing that the Cubans refused to do for themselves. In time, every revolution has created its own mythology, but in this case, these foreign sympathizers, in lieu of embracing one ready-made, had to produce their own. Each of these sympathizers made his own characteristic contribution to this mythology, which, if nothing else, told us what those who felt closest to Castro made of him. The situation was undoubtedly an oddity but, then, the Cuban revolution was an odd one.

THE MYTHMAKERS

One of the first and favorite myths was that of Castro's "peasant revolution." It turned up in the articles written and interviews given by the French writers Jean-Paul Sartre and Simone de Beauvoir, who spent March, 1960, in Cuba. After the usual hectic round of short trips and long talks, Sartre wrote a series of sixteen articles in *France-soir*, subsequently published as a book, *Sartre on Cuba*. In one of them he related how he had informed the Cubans that, like the Chinese, they had made a "peasant revolution." The Cuban reaction, he reported, was divided: The "bearded ones" (the *barbudos;* those who had fought in the mountains) agreed with him; the "unbearded ones" (those who had fought in the resistance movements in the cities) maintained that the peasants had fought little or badly and that the revolution had sprung from the cities.

Mme. de Beauvoir gave a somewhat different version in an interview in *France Observateur*. She said that the petty bourgeoisie had begun by stirring up the urban revolution while the peasants had held back; then, bit by bit, the peasants had joined in, the "immediate interests" of the victorious revolution had become those of the peasant class, and thus "despite its origins, the urban revolution can be considered a peasant revolution."

As a full-fledged theory, however, the Cuban peasant revolution made its appearance in the book *Cuba, Anatomy of a Revolution*, by Leo Huberman and Paul M. Sweezy, editors of the magazine *Monthly Review*. After three weeks in Cuba, they were persuaded that the revolution had succeeded because the peasants as a class had actively joined the rebels and had become "one with the revolutionary army." Fidel Castro appeared to them to be "the embodiment of the revolutionary will and energy of the peasantry." As for the kind of system that this peasant revolution had brought forth, Huberman and Sweezy had "no hesitation in answering: *the new Cuba is a socialist Cuba*."

Six months later, they paid another three-week visit to Cuba. By this time, the Castro regime had nationalized a large part of the Cuban economy. This development caused them to revise their previous estimate—the Cuban revolution was no longer "essentially a peasant revolution" because the working class had finally been "swept" into it. Castro himself had not yet reached the point of calling himself a "Marxist," but the two visitors conferred on him the distinction of having arrived, by virtue of his own "rich experience" and "sharp and fertile mind," at an "unmistakably Marxist" interpretation in a way that would have made Marx himself "proud to acknowledge him as a disciple." Despite Castro's "modesty," however, they heard so much about a socialist Cuba that it had become a "commonplace," in contrast to their first trip, during which no one had spoken to them of Cuba as a socialist country, and socialism was not even included among the revolution's ultimate goals.

And so, in the spring of 1960, a new path to socialism was discovered—a peasant revolution led by the middle-class son of a wealthy landowner. And in the fall of 1960, there was more certainty than ever of the socialist revolution in Cuba because the working class had at last caught up with it.*

Other Castro sympathizers went further. Paul Johnson, of the British weekly *New Statesman*, took a quick look at Cuba and reported that Castro had come to power through a "peasant revolution" but governed through "a genuine dictatorship of the proletariat," expressed through the "arbitrary" rule of one man. In *The New Republic*, Professor Samuel Schapiro, an American academic advocate for Castro, merely limited himself to commenting that "the heart of the revolution, the land reform program, is essentially Marxist." And C. Wright Mills, of Columbia University, made an anthology of all the things that Castro and his closest associates said of themselves, at least as of August, 1960.

Professor Mills's book, *Listen, Yankee!*, is a peculiarly useful and exasperating work. It purports to be "the

* In their book, Huberman and Sweezy devoted less than a page to the working class, compared to pages about the peasantry, and they vaguely suggested far more working-class support for the revolution before 1959 than was actually the case. In part of one sentence elsewhere in the book, however, they admitted that "growing support among urban workers" came to Castro after he took power. In their subsequent article in the *Monthly Review* of December, 1960, they implied the peculiar "backwardness" of the Cuban workers by writing that "the nationalizations of the summer and fall have swept the working class into the revolutionary process."

voice of the Cuban revolutionary," not that of its author. From the conversations I had in Cuba in April, 1960, I can testify that the Castro leaders talked in much the way Mills recorded them. Sometimes the words in the book were so close to those I had heard that I felt I knew the name of the source. To this extent, Mills made himself the vehicle of the purest and most direct propaganda, unlike the others who talked to more or less the same people but passed on in their own name what they had been told. No one ever said "Listen, Yankee!" or "Yankee this" and "Yankee that" to me, but except for this touch of artistic license, I consider these long monologues more or less authentic. Anyone who wants to get the Castro party line of the first half of 1960 most nakedly can get it here.

Nevertheless, Mills put his name to the book and in the last few pages gave the Castro case his personal endorsement. He says that he leaves it to the reader to agree or disagree with the points in it, as if there might be one non-Cuban reader in a hundred or a thousand with the necessary background. A reader has a right to expect that the author should do some work of his own beyond listening only to one side, and that a sociologist would be able at least to give a reasonably accurate report of the social structure of the country. The book as a whole is just as honest and dishonest as any unrelieved propaganda is likely to be, and if Mills merely sought to be a front man for the Castro propaganda machine, he succeeded brilliantly. But is that all that should have been expected of C. Wright Mills?

Mills's Cubans—one never knows where they end and

he begins—are not altogether in agreement with Sweezy and Huberman. First, Mills tells what the revolution was *not*—"not a fight between peasants and landowners, or between wage workers and capitalists—either Cuban or Yankee; nor was it a direct nationalist battle between Cubans and foreigners." It was "not an 'economically determined' revolution—either in its origins or in its sources." Nor was it "a revolution by labor unions or wage workers in the city, or by labor parties, or by anything like that." What was it then? The leaders were "young intellectuals and students from the University of Havana"—they are also called "a few middle-class students and intellectuals"—who made "a lot of first moves for a long time before some of their moves began to pay off." The revolution "really began" when, in one of these moves, "a handful of these young intellectuals really got together with the peasants."

Thus Mills's version contains no nonsense about a "peasant revolution"; it merely claims that the decisive forces in the insurrectionary period were the intellectuals and the peasants, with the former in total command. There is also no nonsense about the workers making the revolution; they are said to have joined in after the victory, and their "revolutionary consciousness" was allegedly aroused only subsequently. At this point, however, mythology takes over, and Mills also has the workers superseding the peasants as a revolutionary force. But the greatest nonsense is written about the middle class. The original "handful" of leaders admittedly came exclusively from that class. Nevertheless, the mythology requires that "the middle classes generally supported the revolution, at least in a passive way, during the insurrectionary period, although as a class they had little to do with making it." I take it this means that most members of the middle class supported the revolution passively or not at all.

Mills also compiled a number of programmatic statements by Castro's group. There was still the old reluctance to be pinned down to anything definite, because a "political system" would hamper the leaders, because very few people cared about it anyway, or because the very lack of a system proved that it was democratic. But this motif slides gently into another one: "We ourselves don't quite know what to call what we are building, and we don't care. It is, of course, socialism of a sort." Or, whatever the system is, the Cubans discovered it all by themselves: "In so far as we are Marxist or Leftist (or Communist, if you will) in our revolutionary development and thought, it is not due to any prior commitment in our ideology. It is because of our own development." Still later in the book, Castro's Cuba becomes "a dictatorship of, by and for the peasants and the workers of Cuba" or "a dictatorship of the people." Mills himself considered Castro's regime to be "a revolutionary dictatorship of the peasants and workers of Cuba" in which one man possessed "virtually absolute power."

All these theories by Sartre and De Beauvoir, Huberman and Sweezy, Johnson and Schapiro, Mills's Cubans and Mills cannot be true, but they have one thing in common—they serve the purpose of concealing the fact that the Cuban revolution was essentially a middle-class revolution that has been used to destroy the middle class.

And without understanding this apparent contradiction, very little can be understood of Castro's Cuba as a social system.

TERROR AND COUNTERTERROR

To begin with, what truth is there in Castro's "peasant revolution"? The core of the eighty-two men under Castro who invaded Cuba from Mexico in December, 1956, and the twelve who found their way to the mountainous Sierra Maestra at the eastern end of the island came from the middle class. At first, the peasants were hostile, and the original twelve dwindled at one time to only nine. Then in March, 1957, Frank País, the underground leader in Santiago de Cuba, sent fifty-eight recruits to the Sierra Maestra, many of them armed with weapons stolen from the U.S. naval base at Guantánamo. These reinforcements, overwhelmingly middle class in character, gave Castro his second wind. Castro himself was their ideal representative—son of a rich landowner, university graduate, lawyer. The *guajiros*, or peasants, in the mountains were utterly alien to most of them. But they had to win the confidence of the peasants to obtain food, to protect themselves from dictator Fulgencio Batista's spies and soldiers, to gain new recruits. As the months passed, the relations between them and the peasants took on a new dimension. The crying poverty, illiteracy, disease, and primitivism of the outcast peasants appalled the young city-bred ex-students. Out of this experience, partly practical and partly emotional, came a determination to revolutionize Cuban society by raising the lowest and most neglected sector to a civilized level of well-being and human dignity.

But, for over a year, Castro's fighting force was so small that he did not expect to overthrow Batista from the mountains. Castro himself described his isolated and near-desperate situation in his letter of December 31, 1957, to the so-called Council of Liberation: "For those who are fighting against an army incomparable in number and in arms, without any support during a whole year other than the dignity with which we are fighting for a cause which we love sincerely and the conviction that it is worth while to die for it, bitterly forgotten by fellow-countrymen who, in spite of having all the ways and means, have systematically (not to say criminally) denied us their help. . . ." Victory was foreseen through the vastly larger resistance movement in the cities, overwhelmingly middle class in composition. This calculation was behind the ill-fated general strike of April 9, 1958. Castro's manifesto of March 12, 1958, read in part: "2. That the strategy of the final stroke should be based on the general revolutionary strike, to be seconded by military action. . . ." It failed because the middle class could not carry off a general strike. Only the workers and trade unions could do so, and they refused mainly for two reasons: They were doing too well under Batista to take the risk, and the official Cuban Communists deliberately sabotaged the strike because they had not been consulted and no attempt was made to reach an agreement with them in advance. The National Committee of the Communist Party, known since the last war as the Partido Socialista Popular (PSP), issued a statement on April 12, 1958, a copy of which I have seen, blaming the fiasco on the "unilateral call" for the strike by the leadership of Castro's 26th of July Movement in Havana under Faustino Pérez.

In the mountains at this time, Mills was told, the armed men under Castro numbered only about 300. Four months later, in August, 1958, the two columns commanded by Majors Guevara and Camilo Cienfuegos, which had been entrusted with the mission of cutting the island in two—the biggest single rebel operation of the entire struggle—amounted, according to Guevara, to 220 men (*Verde Olivo*, October 8, 1960). Sartre was told that the total number of *barbudos* in Cuba during the whole campaign was only 3,000.* Castro's fighting force was until the end so minute that it hardly deserves to be called an army, let alone a "peasant army," and even the influx of the last four or five months failed to give it anything like a mass character. In any case, the character of an army is established by its leadership and cadres, which remained almost exclusively middle class throughout, and not by its common soldiers—or every army in the world would similarly be an army of the peasantry and proletariat.†

* Even this figure may be vastly inflated. The true number was probably closer to 1,000 than to 3,000. But even Sartre's figure serves to make the point.

† The cream of the jest is that Guevara is authority for the statement that the *campesinos* of the Sierra Maestra, from whom the rebel army was first recruited, "came from that part of this social class which shows most aggressively its love for the land and its possession, that is to say, which expresses most perfectly the spirit which can be characterized as petty bourgeois" (*Verde Olivo*, April 9, 1961). Thus, the rebel army was initially made up of the urban and rural petty bourgeoisie, at least in spirit!

[illegible] could such a small band "defeat" Batista's army [illegible] 40,000?

The answer is that it did not defeat Batista's army in any military sense. It succeeded in making Batista destroy himself. Until the spring of 1958, life in most of Cuba went on much as usual. But the fiasco of the April strike forced Castro to change his tactics. Disappointed in his hopes of a mass uprising, he shifted over to full-scale guerrilla warfare—bombings, sabotage, hit-and-run raids. Batista's answer to the terror was counterterror. The army and secret police struck back blindly, indiscriminately, senselessly. The students, blamed as the main troublemakers, were their chief victims. It became safer for young men to take to the hills than to walk in the streets. The orgy of murders, tortures, and brutalities sent tremors of fear and horror through the entire Cuban people and especially the middle-class parents of the middle-class students.

This universal revulsion in the last six months of Batista's rule penetrated and permeated his own army and made it incapable of carrying out the offensive it launched in May against Castro's hideout. As Mills's book says, Batista's army "just evaporated." The engagements between the two sides were so few and inconclusive that Batista's abdication caught Castro by surprise. The real victor in this struggle was not Castro's "peasant army" but the entire Cuban people. The heaviest losses were suffered by the largely middle-class urban resistance movement, which secreted the political and psychological acids that ate into Batista's fighting force; Sartre was told that Batista's army and police killed 1,000 *barbudos* in the last clashes in the mountains and 19,000 in the urban resistance movement.

Castro's guerrilla tactics, then, aimed not so much at "defeating" the enemy as at inducing him to lose his head, fight terror with counterterror on the largest possible scale, and make life intolerable for the ordinary citizen. The same terror that Castro used against Batista has been used against Castro. And Castro has responded with counterterror, just as Batista did.

THE PROMISED LAND

The struggle for power also helps to answer the question: Was the Cuban revolution "betrayed"? The answer obviously depends on what revolution one has in mind—the revolution that Castro promised before taking power, or the one he has made since taking power.

Huberman and Sweezy have written: "Fidel had made his promises and was determined to carry them out, faithfully and to the letter." But neither they, nor Mills, nor Sartre ever says what these promises were. The oversight has been a necessary part of the mythology.

I have made a brief inventory of the promises, political and economic, made by Castro from his "History Will Absolve Me" speech (at his Moncada trial in 1953) to the end of 1958. These promises so soon became embarrassing that some of his literary champions began to rewrite history (after less than two years!) by avoiding all mention of them.

Political

Castro's 1953 speech predicted that the first revolutionary law would be restoration of the 1940 Constitution and made an allusion to a "government of popular election."

Castro's manifesto of July, 1957, his first political declaration from the Sierra Maestra, contained a "formal promise" of general elections at the end of one year and an "absolute guarantee" of freedom of information, press, and all individual and political rights guaranteed by the 1940 Constitution.

Castro's letter of December 14, 1957, to the Cuban exiles upheld the "prime duty" of the post-Batista provisional government to hold general elections and the right of political parties, even during the provisional government, to put forward programs, organize, and participate in the elections.

In an article in *Coronet* magazine of February, 1958, Castro wrote of fighting for a "genuine representative government," "truly honest" general elections within twelve months, "full and untrammelled" freedom of public information and all communication media, and re-establishment of all personal and political rights set forth in the 1940 Constitution. The greatest irony is that he defended himself against the accusation "of plotting to replace military dictatorship with revolutionary dictatorship."

In his answers to his first biographer, Jules Dubois, in May, 1958, Castro pledged "full enforcement" of the 1940 Constitution and "a provisional government of entirely civilian character that will return the country to normality and hold general elections within a period of no more than one year."

In the unity manifesto of July, 1958, Castro agreed "to guide our nation, after the fall of the tyrant, to normality by instituting a brief provisional government that will lead the country to full constitutional and democratic procedures."

ECONOMIC

In the 1953 speech, Castro supported grants of land to small planters and peasants, with indemnification to the former owners; the rights of workers to share in profits; a greater share of the cane crop to all planters; and confiscation of all illegally obtained property. His land reform advocated maximum holdings for agricultural enterprises and the distribution of remaining land to farming families; it also provided for encouragement of "agricultural cooperatives for the common use of costly equipment, cold storage, and a uniform professional direction in cultivation and breeding." In addition, the speech expressed the intention of nationalizing the electric and telephone companies.

The manifesto of July, 1957, defined the agrarian reform as distribution of barren lands, with prior indemnification, and conversion of sharecroppers and squatters into proprietors of the lands worked on.

The *Coronet* article favored a land reform to give peasants clear title to the land, with "just compensation of expropriated owners." It declared that Castro had no plans for expropriating or nationalizing foreign invest-

ments and that he had suspended an earlier program to extend government ownership to public utilities. On nationalization, he wrote:

> I personally have come to feel that nationalization is, at best, a cumbersome instrument. It does not seem to make the state any stronger, yet it enfeebles private enterprise. Even more importantly, any attempt at wholesale nationalization would obviously hamper the principal point of our economic platform—industrialization at the fastest possible rate. For this purpose, foreign investments will always be welcome and secure here.

In May, 1958, he assured Jules Dubois:

> Never has the 26th of July Movement talked about socializing or nationalizing the industries. This is simply stupid fear of our revolution. We have proclaimed from the first day that we fight for the full enforcement of the Constitution of 1940, whose norms establish guarantees, rights, and obligations for all the elements that have a part in production. Comprised therein is free enterprise and invested capital as well as many other economic, civic, and political rights.

The unity manifesto of July, 1958, which was written by Castro, merely called for:

> A minimum governmental program that will guarantee the punishment of the guilty ones, the rights of the workers, the fulfillment of international commitments, public order, peace, freedom, as well as the economic, social, and political progress of the Cuban people.

Law No. 3 of the Sierra Maestra on Agrarian Reform, dated October 10, 1958, on the very eve of taking power, was based on the principle that those who cultivate the land should own it. This law, signed by Fidel Castro and the then Judge Advocate General, Dr. Humberto Sorí Marín, made no mention of "cooperatives" or "state farms." Its entire intent was to implement the hitherto neglected agrarian-reform provision in the Constitution of 1940.*

Such were the promises that Fidel had made.† The near unanimity with which Castro's victory was accepted in January, 1959, was the result not merely of his heroic struggle and glamorous beard but of the political consensus he appeared to embody. This consensus had resulted from the democratic disappointments in 1944–52 and the Batista despotism of 1952–58. There was

* Its full text, which became extremely rare after Castro took power, may be found in Enrique González Pedrero, *La Revolución Cubana* (Mexico: Escuela Nacional de Ciencias Políticas y Sociales, 1959), pp. 143–56.

† Castro's pre-1959 promises are dealt with by Huberman and Sweezy in a peculiar way. They cite twelve and a half pages of the 1953 speech but omit the five-point program on which Castro said the revolution was based. This program began: "The first revolutionary law would have restored sovereignty to the people and proclaimed the Constitution of 1940 as the true supreme law of the state, until such time as the people should decide to modify it or to change it." The others provided for grants of land to small planters and peasants, with indemnification to the former owners; the right of workers to share in profits; a greater share of the cane crop to all planters; and confiscation of all illegally obtained property.

Although the speech makes other important points, this is the only itemized program in it, and it is hard to see how its omission can be justified. The unity pact of July, 1958, is handled in the same way. It contained three points: a common strategy, postwar "normality," and "a minimum governmental program." I have quoted the second point in full in the text. Huberman and Sweezy cite a paragraph in this unity pact that asked the U.S. to cease all military and other types of aid to Batista, but ignore the three-point program, which might have put Castro's promises in a somewhat different light.

Mills simply ignores the whole collection of Castro's prepower pledges.

broad agreement that Cuba could never go back to the corrupt brand of democracy of the past, and the Cuban middle class was ready for deep-going social and political reforms to make impossible another Prío Socarrás and another Batista. Castro promised to restore Cuban democracy and make it work, not a "direct" or "people's" democracy but the one associated with the 1940 Constitution, which was so radical that much of it, especially the provision for agrarian reform, was never implemented.

It is, moreover, unthinkable that Castro could have won power if he had given the Cuban people the slightest forewarning of what he has presented them with—a press and all other means of communication wholly government controlled, ridicule of elections, wholesale confiscation and socialization, "cooperatives" that are (as Huberman and Sweezy admitted) virtually "state farms," or a dictatorship of any kind, including that of the proletariat. It was precisely the kind of promises Castro made that enabled him to win the support of the overwhelming majority of the Cuban middle and other classes; a "peasant revolution" would hardly have been expressed in quite the same way.

The least that can be said, therefore, is that Castro promised one kind of revolution and made another. The revolution Castro promised was unquestionably betrayed.

THE SOCIOLOGICAL IMAGINATION

The Castro mythology tends to distort not only the original nature of the Cuban revolution but also the character of Cuban society. Pages were written by Huberman and Sweezy about the peasantry, a single paragraph about the working class, and almost nothing about the middle class. Mills never seems to have made up his mind which Cubans were speaking through him. His own list of the Cubans who spoke to him indicates that there was not a worker, and certainly not a peasant, in the lot. Without exception, his informants were middle-class intellectuals and professionals of the type in power. Sometimes he makes them speak in their own name; more often they masquerade as the most impoverished and miserable of Cuban peasants. They say, "we squatted on the edge of the road in our filthy huts," as if they were the "we" and as if this was typical of all Cubans. The average reader might imagine that Cuba was nothing but "a place of misery and filth, illiteracy and exploitation and sloth." This may be a triumph of propaganda but it is a travesty of sociology.

Cuba before Castro was, indeed, a country with serious social problems, but it was far from being a peasant country or even a typically "underdeveloped" one. Its population was more urban than rural: 57 per cent lived in the urban areas and 43 per cent in the rural, with the trend strongly in favor of the former (according to the *Geografía de Cuba*, written by Antonio Núñez Jiménez, the first Director of the Agrarian Reform Institute). The people dependent on agriculture for a living made up about 40 per cent, and of these over one-quarter were classified as farmers and ranchers. In 1954, the national income was divided as follows: the sugar industry, agricultural and industrial, 25 per cent; other agriculture,

13 per cent; other industry and commerce, 40 per cent; everything else, 21 per cent. In 1950, only 44 per cent of the total labor force was agricultural.

The standard of living, low by U.S. and West European standards, was comparatively high for Latin America; only three countries, Venezuela, Argentina, and Chile, rated above Cuba in per capita income; Cuba's was almost as high as Italy's and much higher than Japan's. Cuba ranked fifth in Latin America in manufacturing, behind Brazil, Argentina, Mexico, and Chile. Cuba had 1 automobile for every 39 inhabitants (in Argentina, 1 for every 60; in Mexico, 91; in Brazil, 158), and 1 radio for every 5 inhabitants (second to Argentina, with 1 for every 3). Cuban tourists were able to spend more in the United States than American tourists spent in Cuba. After World War II, Cuban interests were strong enough to buy a substantial share of U.S.-owned sugar production, which fell from 70–80 per cent of the total at its high point in the 1930's to about 35 per cent in 1958. Government encouragement of "Cubanization" would easily have cut the figure in half again in a short time under a post-Batista democratic regime.*

I am not trying to suggest that Cuba's economy was a healthy one. It was precariously dependent on the fluctu-

* Cuba was, in fact, an unevenly developed country with a relatively high standard of living, as one of the leading Cuban Communists, Aníbal Escalante, has admitted: "In reality, Cuba was not one of the countries with the lowest standard of living of the masses in America but, on the contrary, one of those with the highest standard of living, and it was here where the first great patriotic, democratic, and socialist revolution of the continent burst forth and where the imperialist chain was first broken. If the historical development had been dictated by the false axiom expressed above, the revolution should have been first produced in Haiti, Colombia, or even Chile, countries of greater poverty for the masses than the Cuba of 1952 or 1958" (*Verde Olivo*, July 30, 1961).

ations of a single crop, sugar, which accounted for more than 80 per cent of Cuban exports and employed about a half million workers for only three to four months a year. As the rates of illiteracy show—41.7 per cent in the rural areas and only 11.6 per cent in the urban areas—the social development of Cuba was shockingly unbalanced in favor of the cities and towns, and Castro's crusade for the peasantry has repaid the Cuban upper and middle classes for decades of indifference to the welfare of the land workers.

But this is not the same thing as implying (as Mills often does) that Cuba was nothing but a land of backward, illiterate, diseased, starving peasants. When he writes, "We speak Spanish, we are mainly rural, and we are poor," the first statement is undoubtedly correct, the second is demonstrably false, and the third is partly true. Cuba was one of the most middle-class countries in Latin America.

In effect, this mythology of the Cuban social structure makes Castro's victory inexplicable. If a "handful" of middle-class "students and intellectuals" had the active support of only a few hundred or even a few thousand peasants, without either the working or middle classes (as Mills maintains), the Batista regime would never have toppled. It was the descrtion of the middle class—on which Batista's power was based—that caused his regime to disintegrate from within and his army to evaporate.

ECLIPSE OF A MOVEMENT

Castro's "betrayal" of the Cuban revolution has also taken another form. When Batista fell, two movements entered into competition—Castro's 26th of July Movement (named after the date of his first unsuccessful attempt, in 1953) and the official Communist Party, the Partido Socialista Popular. The odds seemed to favor the former overwhelmingly. In his first victory address at Camp Liberty, Castro spoke of the popular sympathy and almost unanimous support of the Cuban youth that the 26th of July Movement enjoyed, and he appeared to argue that there was no need for any other movement.

But a different fate soon awaited the 26th of July Movement. The reason, as it was explained to Mme. de Beauvoir, is most revealing:

> The 26th of July Movement, from which the revolution issued, had an apparatus, but a petty-bourgeois one, which could not follow the revolution in the radicalization that has been proceeding since the taking of power; it was not capable of going along with the advance of the agrarian reform. So it was permitted to fall away [*France Observateur*, April 7, 1960].

Mme. de Beauvoir passed on this information without the slightest indication that there might have been something unwholesome in this procedure. But apart from the justification for Castro's decision to eviscerate his own movement, she confirmed the middle-class character of that movement and Castro's political reason for condemning it to a nominal existence—the difference between its revolution and his.

Not so long ago also, there was no higher honor in Castro's Cuba than to belong to the rebel army. It was the chief basis of Castro's rule; army men actually ran the country through ostensibly civilian organizations, such as the Agrarian Reform Institute. When Huberman and Sweezy first visited Cuba, in March, 1960, they reported that "from January 1, 1959, to this day the real power has always been in the revolutionary army, manned and nourished by as radical a social class as any in the world today"—the Cuban peasantry. But on their second visit, six months later, they noted the "(relative) eclipse" of the rebel army and the officially inspired rise of the large, amorphous militia. Indeed, in their December, 1960, article, they no longer referred to it as the rebel army; it had become the "regular army." Instead of the "truly most remarkable relations of solidarity, trust, and understanding" between Castro and the army at the time of their book, they intimated that it had become a potential counterrevolutionary force, typical of Latin American "standing armies." Once the rebel army's peasant character had been its greatest glory; now it had apparently become a serious drawback. In any case, it went the way of the 26th of July Movement.

The fate of David Salvador, the outstanding labor leader of the 26th of July Movement, tells the same story. Before Batista fell, Salvador represented the underground group Labor Unity, and coordinated the resistance within the working class. At a time when the official Cuban Communists opposed Castro as a "putschist," Salvador believed in him and in the last period of Batista's rule went to jail for his underground activity. After the victory, he took over the leadership of the Cuban labor movement for the 26th of July Movement and served as Secretary General of the Cuban Confederation of Labor (Confederación de Trabajadores de Cuba), or CTC. At its national congress in November, 1959, however, Salvador's fortunes suddenly changed. The 26th of July Movement would have scored an overwhelming victory over the Communists, if Fidel Castro himself had not unexpectedly appeared at the congress, berated the delegates for "having given proof neither of prudence, nor of unity, nor of anything," and demanded, in effect, the installation of a triumvirate in the federation's leadership, including the pro-Communist candidate, Jesús Soto. Soon the Communist organ *Hoy* began to attack Salvador openly for his "strange attitude."

With five others, David Salvador was caught in November, 1960, trying to escape from Cuba in a small boat, and he was again cast into prison, this time by Batista's successor, Fidel Castro. The trade unions have lost even the bargaining power they had under Batista; they have become propaganda appendages of the Ministry of Labor, which makes all decisions on wages and conditions, Soviet style.*

What does all this mean? In his own 26th of July Movement, in the rebel army, and in the labor movement, Castro has shunted aside the very ones who helped him in the struggle for power. He has done so, as Mme. de Beauvoir has hinted, because they were led to expect a different revolution from the one he was making. The 26th of July Movement was sacrificed first because it was the embryo of a political party. It could grow into a full-fledged party or become an empty shell. The rebel

* Salvador's story has been told in a pamphlet, *David Salvador—Castro's Prisoner*, by Carlos Rodríguez Quesada, published by the Labor Committee to Release Imprisoned Trade Unionists and Democratic Socialists, New York, 1961.

army has never recovered from the shock of Castro's persecution of one of his closest former comrades-in-arms, Major Hubert Matos, who was sentenced to twenty years' imprisonment for having protested against the favoritism shown to Communists in the army. As Mills remarks in *Listen, Yankee!*, "that was the biggest blow."

The "mass assemblies" and amorphous militias now suited Castro's purposes better because they are so impersonal and anonymous. The individuals in the outdoor spectacles have a direct relationship only to Castro personally, not to each other. The demonstrations are as "democratic" as Hitler's Nuremberg rallies and Mussolini's balcony speeches once were.

The 26th of July Movement and the rebel army were more than Castro's personal emanations; their members were bound by a cause for which they had fought and sacrificed together. That cause went back to a period before Castro's personal rule and to a revolution waged against personal rule. That Castro could not live with the 26th of July Movement and the rebel army is more than faintly reminiscent of Stalin's need to abolish the Society of Old Bolsheviks.

LEMONADE AND REVOLUTION

Lukewarm lemonade helped Jean-Paul Sartre to understand the nature of Castro's "democracy."

One day, as Sartre tells the story, Castro invited Mme. de Beauvoir and himself on an "inspection tour" of Veradero Beach. Soon the party stopped at a little refreshment stand. Castro offered them some lemonade. He started to drink some himself, put down his glass, and said loudly: "It's lukewarm." Then the following dialogue ensued:

> "Don't you have refrigerators?" Castro asked.
>
> "Sure we do," the waitress said. "But they don't work."
>
> "Have you reported it to your superior?"
>
> "Of course, last week. And it isn't a big job," she added familiarly. "An electrician could do it in two hours of work."
>
> "And no one has been ordered to make the repairs?"
>
> She shrugged her shoulders. "You know how it is," she added.

And this is Sartre's comment on the scene:

> It was the first time that I understood—still somewhat vaguely—what I called the other day, "direct democracy." Between the waitress and Castro, an immediate secret understanding [*connivence*] was established. . . .

Castro was not yet satisfied. Sartre relates how Castro insisted on going over to the delinquent refrigerator and vainly tried to fix it himself. At length, Castro turned to the young waitress and muttered:

> "Tell your superiors that if they don't get busy on their problems, they will have problems with me."

One read and wondered. Could it really be that this banal and somewhat embarrassing little scene convinced the famous and worldly French philosopher that Castro's Cuba was, not an ordinary kind of democracy, but a "direct democracy"? Involuntarily, my mind went back to some experiences in the Dominican Republic a few years ago. There, too, the *Líder Máximo*, who preferred being called *El Jefe*, liked to visit his domain, see his subjects personally, and settle problems on the spot. To my dismay, I discovered that there was much to be said for his regime in purely physical terms, that the peasants worshiped him, that he could have won honest elections quite as overwhelmingly as his fixed elections, and that the only ones who seemed disturbed were a few intellectuals and other dubious middle-class characters. It was easy to imagine the same scene played by *El Jefe*, the young waitress, lukewarm lemonade, and the refrigerator that wouldn't work, except perhaps that *El Jefe*, having had much more time, no longer permitted lukewarm lemonade under any circumstances. But the greatest blow of all came one day when I entered into a philosophical discussion with a leading official and asked whether *El Jefe's* unique system had a name. Gravely and courteously, he answered: "neodemocracy." I must have flushed in anger. If only they would leave "democracy" alone! If Generalissimo Rafael Leónidas Trujillo was the leader of a democracy, even a "neodemocracy," who was not?

At bottom, all these "neo" and "direct" democracies rest on a simple proposition: that the Leader and his people are one and indivisible. Hence they need no representative institutions, no elections, no loyal or disloyal oppositions, no free or partially critical press, none of the rights and safeguards traditionally associated with a democracy.

The horror of this thinking is that it wipes out the lessons to be learned from the most desperate and tragic experiences of our time. If there is anything that should have burned itself into our consciousness, it is the excruciating evil of the popular despot, the beloved dictator, the mass leader. The *connivence* that Sartre imagined between Castro and the waitress existed between Hitler and a too large portion of the German people and between Trujillo and an even larger portion of the Dominican people. More horrible still is the fact that, with the whole modern machinery of propaganda at their disposal, the Leaders can manufacture a reasonable facsimile of popular consent even if they may not have it to start out with. Is it necessary at this late date to recall these terrible lessons to Jean-Paul Sartre? Could he have survived the "direct democracy" that he recommends to the Cubans?

Castro's "democracy" posed awkward problems for all his apologists. Their argument ran: (a) Castro could win any election overwhelmingly and, therefore, (b) elections were unnecessary or harmful and, anyway, (c) all previous Cuban elections were crooked. Here, again, it seems necessary to recall the ABC's of democracy to people who pride themselves on being the only real democrats. The democratic mandate is not one that once given cannot be revoked; it is of the essence of democratic consent that it must be periodically renewed.

There were three stages in Castro's attitude toward elections. First, he promised them. Then he said they were not immediately feasible. Finally, he ridiculed them. In effect, he once said: "Cuba has never had an honest election and a truly free press. I will show Cuba how to have them." Later, he said: "Cuba has never had an honest election and a truly free press. Therefore, Cuba has no right to have them under me." Here, in essence, were the two revolutions of Fidel Castro.*

The problem of elections was evaded by the counter-offer of something even better. Huberman and Sweezy wrote: "What we do maintain is that the revolution itself gives the Government a far more democratic mandate than the freest of free elections ever could, and that it is the sacred duty of the Government to *carry out* the oft-announced platform of the revolution before it comes back to the people asking for either approval or further instructions." What revolution? What platform? The revolution to restore the Constitution of 1940 and hold elections in twelve to eighteen months? Or the revolution against the Constitution and against elections for an indefinite period? How could the Government come *back* to the people for "approval" and "further instructions" when it has never once gone to them for approval or instructions?

The reference to the "oft-announced platform of the revolution" is simply incredible. Huberman and Sweezy might have been less tempted to make it if they had not successfully avoided stating that platform. They themselves tell a story that belies it. According to them, the first draft of the agrarian-reform law contained no provision for cooperatives. All the revolutionaries around Castro believed that the peasants were not ready for them. The decision to have them was made by Castro

* I mean by "two revolutions" not what Fidel Castro may have inwardly believed or intended but what his movement openly and concretely stood for. The dispute over whether Castro "betrayed" or "deceived" his followers is, to my mind, a profitless one; more to the point is what he said and what he did.

alone against the better judgment of his closest advisers and adherents.* By Huberman and Sweezy's own admission, then, Castro did not carry out "the oft-announced platform of the revolution" as anyone else had understood it in this key area; he carried out a basic revision of that platform to the surprise of everyone but Fidel Castro.

The present-day Cuban "cooperatives" are usually traced back to Castro's "History Will Absolve Me" speech, in 1953. A careful reading of the key passage in that speech hardly bears this out:

> A revolutionary government, after transferring the ownership of parcels of land to the 100,000 small farmers who today pay rent, would proceed to a definite solution of the land problem by, first: establishing, as the Constitution orders, a maximum acreage for each type of agricultural enterprise and acquiring

* Some intriguing details of this story were volunteered by Fidel Castro in his speech on December 20, 1961. It seems that "the 'cooperative' concept was introduced in the agrarian-reform law" in a discussion on a plane! The question arose whether the land should be given outright or in usufruct. Castro decided on "ownership of the land of the cooperative" in the law, but he never intended to give the cooperatives anything but usufruct, "so that enemies should not be able to take advantage" of the language. As he remarked, "no one would understand the agrarian reform by studying the agrarian law," because the law said one thing and he intended it to mean another—a characteristically *Fidelista* tactic. It may well be that the plane trip to which he refers was the one made to the Sierra Maestra to proclaim the law (*Revolución*, December 22, 1961). I have been told by then members of his Cabinet that the ministers were totally ignorant of the agrarian-reform law before it was suddenly submitted to them, that it had been drawn up by a small group responsible to Castro alone, and that he expected the Cabinet to sign it without even having read it. The whole thing was put through so precipitately that the members of the government signed it with only the vaguest notion of what was in it. Under protest, at one Cabinet meeting, Castro began to read the long, complex document but never finished.

> the excess acreage by means of expropriation, recovering lands usurped from the state, filling in swamp- and marshlands, planting vast tracts, and reserving zones for reforestation; second, distributing the remaining land among farming families with preference given to the largest ones, encouraging agricultural cooperatives for the common use of costly equipment, cold storage, and a uniform professional direction in cultivation and breeding, and, finally, to facilitate assistance, equipment, protection, and useful knowledge to the farming population [*Pensamiento Político, Económico y Social de Fidel Castro* (Havana: Editorial Lex, 1959), pp. 44–45].

I have purposely translated this passage in its literal form in order to give the reader a sense of where cooperatives belonged in the total scheme of Castro's 1953 agricultural policy. They obviously occupied a minor place in the general scheme; they were intended, in the traditional meaning of cooperatives, to service independent landowners. These 1953 cooperatives were clearly not the "state farms" of 1959. In addition, Castro seems to have dropped or rarely mentioned "cooperatives" after 1953.

The version of this passage in the Huberman-Sweezy book (p. 41) is taken from the official English translation of this speech, published by the Liberal Press, New York. For some reason, the phrase "for the common use of costly equipment, cold storage" was omitted from this translation, as a result of which the whole section on cooperatives is somewhat distorted. In 1953, Castro's "agrarian reform" meant what it has usually meant: land for landless peasants. But, then, Huberman and Sweezy discovered, via a translator, that Cuban peasants do not want their own land; they did not even understand the question of owning their own land "until it had been repeatedly rephrased and explained" (p. 116 n.). Huberman and Sweezy add that this incident set them off on their entire interpretation of the Cuban revolution! If so, the Cuban peasants are truly unique, and no one apparently ever understood them before—certainly not Fidel Castro, who put so much emphasis on giving them their own land in 1953 and after.

But there is something even more deeply objectionable in the Huberman-Sweezy reasoning. It implies that anyone who claims to possess the true idea of the revolution confers on himself a more democratic mandate than any that the people, even in the freest of free elections, can give him. The next step, and revolutionists have taken it, is to say that it is "democratic" to make the revolution without the people or despite the people—in, of course, the people's interest. Out of such revolutions have invariably come the worst tyrannies.

SCAPEGOAT HISTORY

While some writers saw everything but Communism in Castro, others saw nothing but Communism. The most extreme version of this second school of thought may be found in the book *Red Star Over Cuba*, by Nathaniel Weyl. Weyl knew the international Communist movement from the inside during the 1930's—he has testified that he once belonged to the same American Party unit as Alger Hiss—and he has also written a book on Mexico's agrarian reform under ex-President Lázaro Cárdenas. There is no indication, however, that he has a personal knowledge of Cuba.

Much of Weyl's book is based on police and intelligence sources, such as the Batista regime's Bureau for the Repression of Communist Activities (BRAC). A lurid series of articles in a sensation-mongering New York tabloid is treated as if it were a serious historical source. The recklessness with which Weyl uses his materials, good, bad, and dubious, is matched by that of his views. These range from the conviction that Fidel Castro has been "a trusted Soviet agent" since 1948, when he was little more than twenty-one years old, to the imputation that Cuba was lost to Communism by "appeasement-oriented" officials of the State Department. The implicit thesis of the book was stated by Senators James Eastland and Thomas Dodd of the Senate Internal Security Subcommittee, whom Weyl quotes: "Cuba was handed to Castro and the Communists by a combination of Americans in the same way that China was handed to the Communists." In effect, this is the extreme Right-wing case against Castro and those who allegedly put him into power.

Weyl's methods hardly inspire confidence in his results. He makes some members of the State Department the butt of his indignation for having failed to accept the evidence that Castro has been a Communist and Soviet agent for a dozen years. But, for some reason, he fails to mention that General C. P. Cabell, Deputy Director of the U.S. Central Intelligence Agency, testified in November, 1959, before the Senate Internal Security Subcommittee (one of Weyl's favorite sources) that "we believe that Castro is not a member of the Communist Party, and does not consider himself to be a Communist." Presumably, the CIA had gone to some trouble to find out all about Castro's past political allegiances and was less riddled than the State Department with "appeasement-minded subordinates" (Weyl's phrase for then Under Secretary Christian A. Herter, Assistant Secretary for Latin American Affairs Roy R. Rubottom, and Director of the Caribbean Division William A. Wieland). The CIA may have been wrong, but its evaluation of the evidence certainly has a bearing on Weyl's case against members of the State Department with a similar view.

Weyl, however, cites the testimony before the Senate Internal Security Subcommittee of Rafael Díaz Balart (Castro's former brother-in-law), who worked for Batista to the end. He writes that Díaz Balart gave "basically the same account" as that of Dr. Emilio Núñez Portuondo, Batista's former Prime Minister, who declared that "Fidel Castro subordinated himself to Communist Party discipline during his first year at the University (1945–46) and used his Party name of Fidelio." Weyl then quotes those portions of Díaz Balart's testimony which indicate that Castro and the Communist students had had "a very nice understanding" about helping each other. But he does not quote Díaz Balart's direct assertion: "No, he was not in that moment a member. He was just in that moment an opportunist leader who wanted to promote himself." Basically, Díaz Balart gave anything but the same account as Núñez Portuondo.

Weyl also plays fast and loose in his references to

Communist money allegedly put at Castro's disposal in the Sierra Maestra. He quotes from the articles by two newspapermen in the New York *Daily News:* " 'Once,' said a man who was close to Fidel, 'Carlos Rafael Rodríguez, an active member of the Communist party in Cuba, arrived with a dozen men loaded with money. It came to $800,000 and Fidel hugged him and shouted, "Now we're ready to win the war." ' " Thus Weyl quotes two newspapermen who quote "a man who was close to Fidel." But some thirty pages later, Weyl writes: "We have seen that Carlos Rafael Rodríguez, who was not only a member of the Political Bureau of the Cuban Communist party, but its brains, went to the Sierra Maestra to bring Fidel Castro almost a million dollars." There is no doubt about Carlos Rafael's journeys to the Sierra Maestra in 1958—he readily admitted them to me when I talked to him in 1960 but only a reader with a short memory would "have seen" that Carlos Rafael had brought Fidel Castro almost a million dollars. Perhaps he did, but the evidence is third-hand at best. Nevertheless, Weyl goes on to assert that "Fidel Castro's forces won primarily because they had almost unlimited supplies of money."

How much more complex Cuban politics can be than Weyl appears to make it may be gathered from his reference to Raúl Roa. Weyl writes that one of the Cuban Communist Party's "charter members and early leaders was Raúl Roa, whom Fidel Castro would later appoint Foreign Minister of Cuba." That is all. From this a reader might suppose that Roa was just another Communist functionary in Castro's entourage. But Roa has had a rather more varied political career. He wrote an article in Mexico in 1956 denouncing "the crimes, disasters, and outrages perpetrated" by the Soviet "invaders" in Hungary. This article, together with other uncomplimentary references to Communism, were reprinted in his book, *En Pie*, issued by an official publishing house in Cuba in October, 1959. The Communist leader Blas Roca, in the official Communist organ *Hoy* of March 11, 1959, denounced Roa as a *plattista*—the historical equivalent of an "agent of American imperialism."* Yet Roa has become a servile spokesman of the Communism and Soviet Union that he had many times condemned.

Weyl also identifies Faustino Pérez as a Communist on the basis of Batista's sources. The official Cuban Communists have always blamed Pérez (the leader of the former Havana underground) for the failure of the April, 1958, strike on the ground that he refused to make a deal with them. They took their revenge in November, 1959, when he was ousted from Castro's government for protesting against the treatment of Major Hubert Matos. Weyl even cites a "Cuban underground" report that Matos worked for the Communists "as early as 1957," without saying a word about the price Matos has paid for his anti-Communism. Such blunders are inevitable in a book that accepts Batista's and Trujillo's sources uncritically. Communists, ex-Communists, non-Communists, and op-

* Senator Orville H. Platt gave his name to the famous amendment that empowered the U.S. to intervene in Cuba; it was revoked in 1934. The Platt Amendment was written into the Cuban Constitution as an appendix in 1901 and embodied in the U.S.-Cuban treaty of 1903. Weyl manages in a single sentence (p. 55 n.) to get Senator Platt's first name and the date of his amendment wrong—a curious feat for a student of Cuba.

portunists are indiscriminately lumped together. Every bit of evidence that does not fit the book's thesis is ruthlessly suppressed or glossed over. All the hard problems of Castro's political developments are oversimplified and vulgarized.

Sometimes a reader of both the Mills and Weyl books might be hopelessly puzzled. Mills's Yankee is taunted with the question, "What did you do—about the weapons, for example, the Yankee Government kept sending —and sending—and sending—to Batista?" But in Weyl's book, former Ambassador Earl E. T. Smith says of the United States decision to stop sending arms to Batista in March, 1958, that "the psychological impact on the morale of the government was crippling." In his recent book, *Respuesta* (*Reply*), published in Mexico, Fulgencio Batista also complains bitterly about the harmful effect of the U.S. embargo on arms. A reader of Mills's book would never know that the arms had ever been cut off. A reader of Weyl's book would never know that the effect of the arms embargo was partially undone by the failure to withdraw the military mission.*

Weyl's chief American scapegoat is Herbert L. Matthews of *The New York Times*. In February, 1957,

* In any case, U.S. military aid to Cuba was relatively modest. From July 1, 1945, to June 30, 1960, U.S. military aid to Cuba and six other Latin American countries amounted to: Cuba, $10.6 million; Uruguay, $23.2 million; Colombia, $25.7 million; Venezuela, $38 million; Chile, $39.7 million; Peru, $51.2 million; Brazil, $152.5 million (*The New York Times*, May 22, 1961). After the U.S. arms embargo of March, 1958, Batista obtained planes and tanks from Great Britain. The military-assistance agreement between the U.S. and Cuba was signed during the administration of Prío Socarrás in 1950, before Batista's coup two years later. The military mission was based on this pre-Batista agreement.

Matthews published three partially misleading articles and photographs, which, however, proved that Castro was alive, and he vouched for Castro's idealism, courage, and innocence of Communism. The chief count against William Wieland seems to be that he advised the newly appointed Ambassador Smith to be briefed by Matthews before assuming his post. Rubottom's main misdeed appears to have been that he told a Senate subcommittee on December 31, 1958, the day before Batista's flight, that "there was no evidence of any organized Communist element within the Castro movement or that Señor Castro himself was under Communist influence." As if this were not trouble enough for Rubottom, he also stands accused of having been the protégé of Dr. Milton Eisenhower, whom Weyl brushes off as "a well-intentioned, vaguely Leftist, former New Deal bureaucrat."

Ambassador Smith's briefing by Matthews, which for a while promised to become a minor *cause célèbre* in some circles of American politics, runs true to form in Weyl's book. On checking, I found that Ambassador Smith had testified: "I spent six weeks in Washington, approximately four days of each week, visiting various agencies and being briefed by the State Department and those whom the State Department designated." He also said that "in the course of six weeks I was briefed by numbers of people in the usual course as every Ambassador is briefed." One of these people, suggested by Wieland, was Matthews. Weyl converts this testimony to: "Ambassador Smith made the remarkable disclosure that Wieland sent him to none other than Herbert Matthews to get his briefing on Cuban affairs before departing for his post in Havana." Thus "a" briefing is transformed into "his" briefing, as if Matthews were the only one to brief Smith. And it is hard to understand what is remarkable about the recommendation of Matthews in May, 1957, among many others, since at the time he was one of the very few Americans who had talked to Fidel Castro.

Some other testimony before the Senate Internal Security Subcommittee, which Weyl does not quote, might not have been irrelevant. According to Batista's commander in the Sierra Maestra area, Colonel Ugalde Carrillo, his forces there numbered 6,000–7,000. He estimated Castro's men at 700–800. In addition, Batista's army contained more than 33,000 men elsewhere. This force of over 40,000 had for years obtained as much arms as it had wanted from the United States and other countries. The American Ambassador from 1953 to the middle of 1957, Arthur Gardner, was so "pro-Batista" that, as Mrs. Ruby Hart Phillips (the long-time *New York Times* correspondent in Havana) wrote in her book, *Cuba: Island of Paradox,* the dictator was embarrassed because he thought that the Ambassador was overdoing it. Despite Matthews' remarkable briefing, Gardner's successor, Earl Smith, was so "anti-Castro" that his subordinates pleaded with him in vain to be less partisan. And despite Matthews' pro-Castro articles of February, 1957, Castro's entire force fourteen months later numbered as few as 300 (according to Mills) and at most 800 (according to Ugalde).*

* Fidel Castro has since revealed that he had only 180 men in April, 1958 (*Revolución,* December 2, 1961; 2d ed.).

The forces at Batista's disposal were to the very end so superior in numbers and weapons that only a vast popular revulsion can account for Batista's debacle. Batista's Chief of Staff, General Francisco Tabernilla, came much closer to the truth when he was asked whether the army could have successfully resisted Castro's march on Havana. "It could," he replied, "but not for a long time, because by that time, the people of Cuba were already against the regime of Batista, and there is no army, once the people get up in arms, that can suppress it."

WHOSE REVOLUTION?

On one thing Mills, Johnson, and Weyl almost agreed. For Mills, Castro's regime was "a revolutionary dictatorship of the peasants and workers." For Johnson, it was a "genuine dictatorship of the proletariat." For Weyl, it was "a dictatorship of the proletariat." What could these long-suffering, ill-defined words mean in relation to Cuba today?

Never has a single one of Castro's ministers been a peasant or proletarian. During my visit to Cuba in 1960, I was curious to find out how far the middle-class background of the government went. It was not an easy task because most members of the Cabinet, a fair sampling of the top leadership, preferred to be known as majors or captains of the former rebel army. Finally I prevailed on one of the ministers to write out on his own stationery the professions or occupations and ages of each one.

Here is the list, as he drew it up in his own handwriting, which I thought interesting enough to keep:

Osvaldo Dorticós. PRESIDENT. *Lawyer*. 40 years.
Fidel Castro. PRIME MINISTER. *Lawyer*. 33.
Augusto Martínez Sánchez. LABOR. *Lawyer*. 34.
Raúl Roa. FOREIGN AFFAIRS. *Professor*. 53.
Osmany Cienfuegos. PUBLIC WORKS. *Architect*. 30–31.
Armando Hart. EDUCATION. *Lawyer*. 29.
Raúl Castro. ARMY. *University student*. 29.
Raúl Cepero Bonilla. COMMERCE. *Lawyer*. 39.
Regino Botí. ECONOMY. *Lawyer*. 36–37.
Rolando Díaz Astaraín. FINANCE. *Naval captain (Academy)*. 3–(?).
Julio Camacho. TRANSPORTATION. *Mayor*. 34.
Serafín Ruiz de Zarate. PUBLIC HEALTH. *Medicine*. 35.
Pedro Miret. AGRICULTURE. *Engineering student*. 32.
José Naranjo. INTERIOR. *Medical student*. 30.
Raquel Pérez. SOCIAL WELFARE. *Philosophy*. 31–32.
Enrique Oltuski. COMMUNICATIONS. *Engineer*. 29.
Alfredo Yabur. JUSTICE. *Lawyer*. 35.
Luis Buch. MINISTER. *Lawyer*. 47.

Most of them still hold the same offices or have been replaced by people of the same type. Every one attended a university (some in the United States), came from an upper- or middle-class home, and became or aspired to become a professional or intellectual. Not a single one represented in any conceivable sense the peasantry or proletariat, or owed his position to its organized strength or pressure. What they were they owed solely to Fidel Castro, and they were responsible to him alone. This much was recognized by Mills who flatly stated that Castro possessed "virtually absolute power" in Cuba. But where does that leave the "dictatorship of the peasants and workers"?

Reflecting on the situation as they saw it in the spring

of 1960, Huberman and Sweezy gave the peasantry the decisive role in the victorious revolution, made Castro the "embodiment of the revolutionary will and energy of the peasantry," and extolled the Cuban peasantry as "perhaps one of the world's most deeply revolutionary classes" and "as radical a social class as any in the world today." Six months later, they returned to Cuba and discovered that the peasantry had been superseded as the "most revolutionary class" by the working class and that the peasant-manned and -nourished rebel army had suffered a relative eclipse. They were delighted in the spring and they were enchanted in the fall; the peasant revolution was wonderful and the swift dispossession of the peasant revolution was even more so. But why the peasantry should have been superseded if it really was "as radical a social class as any in the world today," they did not try to explain. Is it conceivable that the class which had really made the revolution, which the *Líder Máximo* embodied, and which was perhaps the most deeply revolutionary class in the world today would permit itself to be pushed into the background without a word of protest or token of resistance? Is this the behavior of a class toward *its* revolution?

The process thus conjured up was clearly mythological. Those who "gave" the revolution to the peasantry could also take it away. The peasantry never had in its hands any of the levers of command of the revolution, before or after the victory. The revolution was made and always controlled by declassed sons and daughters of the middle class, first in the name of the entire people, then of the peasants, and finally of the workers and peasants.

At most the revolution may be doing things *for* and *to* the peasants and workers. The good and evil in these things may be open to debate, but *who* decides these things and to what class they belong are not. For Marx, the notion that the peasants would have been the driving force of a socialist revolution would have been simply unthinkable; the idea that the working class would have to be "swept" into a socialist revolution after it had been made by another class and as a mechanical result of nationalization from above, equally so.

The alleged role of the working class in this revolution is just as fanciful as that attributed to the peasantry. In December, 1960, a few hundred authentic proletarians employed by the Cuban Electric Company staged a protest march from union headquarters to the Presidential Palace. The rank and file was discontented because the new management of the nationalized electric company had cracked down on privileges long tolerated under the dictatorship and thereby had reduced its standard of living. The leadership, headed by an old 26th of July militant, was enraged because the Cuban Confederation of Labor (now completely controlled by the Communists) had moved to oust it. The revolt was quelled, and the chief union leader, Amaury Fraginals, went underground. In a long, angry speech, Prime Minister Castro admitted that a large part not only of the electrical workers but of the mass of workers in general was "confused." He scorned those who would exchange "the right of the working class to govern and direct the country for a plate of lentils." At one point, he declared: "Do you know what is the first goal for which the working class should fight, the only goal for which a working class in a modern country should fight fundamentally? For the conquest of political power!"

This speech was noteworthy for the political vocabulary employed for the first time by Castro, but it told much more about him than about the Cuban proletariat. Would it be necessary to exhort the proletariat to take power in a "dictatorship *of* the proletariat"? And if it followed his advice, would all the lawyers in Castro's government remain in power? Of all the dictatorships of the proletariat that have been bestowed on us in this century, Castro's is surely the least convincing.

Events also dealt unkindly with Jean-Paul Sartre's clairvoyance. In the introduction (dated September 12, 1960) to the Brazilian edition of his series of articles on Cuba, he wrote: "No, if Cuba desires to separate from the Western bloc, it is not through the crazy ambition of linking itself to the Eastern bloc." He also communicated his certainty that "its objective is not to strengthen one bloc to the detriment of the other." On December 10, 1960, Major Guevara was "crazy" enough to announce publicly in Moscow: "We had no part in drawing up this declaration [of eighty-one Communist Parties], but we support it wholeheartedly" (*Hoy*, December 11, 1960). It would be hard to imagine any way of linking Cuba more closely to the Eastern bloc or of strengthening that bloc to the detriment of the West than the wholehearted support of this declaration.

The attitude of Paul Johnson, in the *New Statesman* of September 17, 1960, toward Latin America in general and Cuba in particular smacked of a peculiar kind of anticolonial colonialism. For him, their basic economic problems could not be solved "through mere electoral victories, since effective legislation requires the assent of the armed forces." Therefore, only *Fidelismo* or Communism—which he regarded as "natural enemies"—remained as practical alternatives. In the case of Cuba, he seemed to have cut the ground under his own argument since the armed forces had disappeared and the need for their assent had vanished with them. The main theme of Castro's "History Will Absolve Me" speech of 1953 and of all his statements until he assumed power was that Cuba's social and economic problems could be solved within the framework of the Constitution of 1940. But there was one thing the Constitution excluded—the dictatorship of a *Líder Máximo* and his junta. The colonialists used to say that some peoples were not fit for anything but some form of imperialism; the anticolonial colonialists say that some peoples are not fit for anything but some form of totalitarianism.

In the end, one wonders how far such words as "socialism," "democracy," "Marxism," and "dictatorship of the proletariat" can be stretched. For some of Castro's admirers, it is clear, they can be stretched to the point of meaninglessness.

Six years ago, for example, Huberman and Sweezy were shocked by Nikita Khrushchev's exposé at the Soviet Communist Party's Twentieth Congress of his predecessor's vices. After a suitable period of reflection and repentance, they came up with a theory of Stalinism as "good ends with bad means." They explained that Stalinism "became the instrument of the advance to socialism" but, unhappily, "incorporated the methods of oriental despotism—murder, mendacity, duplicity, brutality, and above all arbitrariness" (*Monthly Review*, July–August, 1956, pp. 71–72). This view of Stalinism has its roots in a certain conception of socialism. In this conception all that essentially matters is that the economy should be nationalized. The nationalizing state may be murderous, mendacious, guilty of duplicity, brutal, and arbitrary, but it is still "socialist." And by separating the ends from the means, the political from the economic, what the state controls from who controls the state, socialism can be arrived at through oriental despotisms or pseudo-peasant revolutions.

THE CUBAN VARIANT

Marxian socialism was predicated not merely on a nationalized economy but on the harmonious development of several factors. The achievement of economic democracy by the socialist revolution presupposed the achievement of political democracy by the bourgeois-democratic revolution. For this reason, the classical Marxists took political democracy for granted, as we no longer can, and they assumed that economic democracy would be built on it. They conceived of socialism as the culmination of capitalist development, without which the prerequisites of socialism—an advanced industrial economy and a preponderant, impoverished, class-conscious proletariat—could not be fulfilled.

History has not worked out that way. Where capitalism has been successful, the prerequisite of a preponderant, impoverished, class-conscious proletariat has not been fulfilled; and where capitalism has not been successful, the prerequisite of an advanced industrial economy has also not been fulfilled. Either the middle class has not been strong enough to achieve a viable capitalist economy, or it has been strong enough to bar the way to a socialist economy.

This familiar dilemma of modern socialism has spawned all sorts of bastard and spurious "socialisms." Instead of the proletariat, they issue out of the middle class, but of that part in revolt against the shortcomings of the middle class. These sons and daughters of the bourgeoisie gravitate irresistibly toward the ideology of socialism, but they can make use only of those aspects of socialism which conditions permit them to utilize. They cannot be faithful to the fundamental ideas of the socialist tradition —that the proletariat should liberate itself, that there are prerequisites of socialism, especially an advanced industrial economy, and that socialism must fulfill and complement political democracy.

But there is one aspect of socialism on which they can seize without delay or restraint. They can find in Marxism an ideological sanction for the unrestricted and unlimited use of the state to change the social order, and they can find in Leninism a sanction for *their* unrestricted and unlimited power over the state. In classical Marxism, the role of the socialist state was conditioned by the stage of development at which it was put into effect and by the class relationships that governed its realization. In this caricature of socialism, however, the only prerequisite that really matters is the seizure of power, no matter by whom, how, when, or where. Thus we live in a time not only of "Cuban socialism" but of "Indonesian socialism" and even of "African socialism."

This phenomenon indicates that we are badly in need of new words to assume some of the burden that has been thrust on socialism. The order of development cannot be inverted–first the revolution, then the prerequisites of socialism–without resulting in a totally different kind of social order, alien to the letter and, infinitely more, to the spirit of socialism. These inverted revolutions from above belong to what, for want of a better word, we must call the Communist family of revolutions, which, in practice, serve to industrialize the peasantry rather than to liberate the proletariat. But even this family has grown so large and now covers so much ground that its name does not necessarily guarantee full understanding.

For about thirty years, the only Communism was Russian Communism and, in effect, Communism was whatever the Russians said it was. Then, in 1948, came the Titoist variant–a small Communist state in rebellion against Russian domination–and, at the end of 1949, the Chinese variant–a Communist state so vast that it could rival Soviet Russia in power. But both the Yugoslav and Chinese Communist leaderships derived from a common source, the Comintern, which from 1919 to 1943 was tightly controlled by and wholly dependent on the Russian Communists. Thus far the line of descent was clear and direct.

Now a new branch of the family has begun to emerge. It is related to the national-revolutionary movements, which the world Communist movement long before

Khrushchev had recognized as a distinct force and with which it had sometimes collaborated and sometimes competed. As late as 1954, the Soviet press attacked Ghana's President Kwame Nkrumah and his party as a "screen" for British imperialism. Under Khrushchev, however, the pendulum has swung over to the outermost limits of collaboration. This policy, apparently one of the points at issue between the Russian and Chinese Communist Parties, reflects the undeniable fact of the last few years that no Communist has been a match for Nkrumah in Ghana, Sékou Touré in Guinea, or Fidel Castro in Cuba. The local Communists were, therefore, advised to bide their time and achieve their goal in two stages instead of one. First the national-revolutionary movement could win power, then the Communists could win power in the national-revolutionary movement.

This strategy owes its success to a shrewd assessment of the national-revolutionary movements. They are far more capable than the Communists of achieving national unity against the common enemy. But the common enemy, not a social and political program, gives them their *raison d'être*. As a result, they are much more inspiring and effective before taking power than they are afterward. Filling the political and social vacuum the day after the revolution gives the Communists greater opportunities than they had during the revolution. Above all, the nationalist leaders are usually men whose magnetic mass appeal is combined with intellectual fuzziness, adventurist temperaments, and insatiable egos. Their strong appeal makes them indispensable, and their weak points make them vulnerable, to the Communists. They serve the

Communists only on condition that the Communists should appear to be serving them. Their political school was nothing like the Comintern, and they represent a variant still further away from the Russian prototype than Marshal Tito or Mao Tse-tung.

This variant has gone further in Cuba than anywhere else, though the story is far from finished there, too. For this reason, Fidel Castro has cast such a large shadow from such a small island.

The phenomenon of Fidel Castro has, as yet, received little serious study. His revolution may not be the one that he promised to make, but it is for all that a genuine revolution. It is related to other upheavals in countries with similar national and social resentments and inequalities. It cannot be dismissed as nothing more than a diabolical aberration because it is not what it claims to be. It belongs to a new type of system, neither capitalist nor socialist, that emerges where capitalism has not succeeded and socialism cannot succeed. In most pro- and anti-Castro propaganda, the revolution that brought him into power is so ruthlessly distorted that his entire political development begins and ends in fantasy. The serious student will seek answers to questions that the mythologists of "Left" and "Right" do not even ask. How could a revolution basically middle class in nature be turned against that class?* How could a revolution made with-

* I do not use "middle class" in the classical Marxian sense of an antifeudal bourgeois revolution. I use "middle class" in the more ordinary sense of a leadership that derived from middle-class families and followed a middle-class way of life. Cuba had already had its bourgeois revolution, but it was a partially unfulfilled one. This is no place for an extended "class" analysis of the Cuban revolution, if one can as yet be made. My own view, in brief, is that the main

out the official Communists, and for the most part despite them, become so intimately linked with them? How, in short, could Fidel Castro promise one revolution and make another, and what consequences flowed from this revolutionary schizophrenia?

The answers, as I have suggested, take us into territory that has been as yet hardly explored. For the Communists and the *Fidelistas* to meet, *both* had to travel some distance from their starting points. The Communists had to make up their minds that they could win power, not against Fidel, but only through Fidel. In all probability, this decision was made after an internal struggle in the first half of 1958 and carried out in the second half.

Evidence for this view has accumulated. The Communist leader Aníbal Escalante wrote in the official monthly organ, *Fundamentos*, of August, 1959, that the top leadership made a decision in February, 1958, which amounted to a dual policy of supporting an armed struggle in the countryside and a civil struggle in the

---

drive in the struggle for power came from the middle class, especially its younger generation, with other classes providing additional mass support. After the seizure of power, however, the formerly pro-Castro middle-class adherents and sympathizers divided so much that the mass basis changed, though the "class" character of the leadership did not. Boris Goldenberg, who observed the Cuban scene at close range for twenty years, has proposed what may be a particularly fruitful type of analysis. He has called the 26th of July Movement "a group of youths of middle-class origin, with a heroic leader, much faith and little ideological clarity." He considers it "erroneous to characterize the Cuban revolution as the expression of a particular social class," but "it does not for that reason lack a sociological base. This latter is formed by the enormous and heterogeneous mass of the economically 'rootless' "—from all classes ("El desenvolvimiento de la revolución cubana," *Cuadernos*, January–February, 1961, pp. 34–35). In a forthcoming book on the Cuban revolution in relation to the development of Latin America as a whole, Mr. Goldenberg has worked out his views in greater detail.

cities. Escalante cites this decision as the turn toward Communist collaboration with the 26th of July Movement.* Another Communist leader, Carlos Rafael Rodríguez, wrote in the French Communist organ *France Nouvelle* of July 17–23, 1958, that the Cuban Communists were then negotiating with the Castro movement in the trade-union field, "which represents considerable progress toward general political unity." And a third Communist leader, Ursinio Rojas, divulged in *Fundamentos* of March, 1959, that these trade-union-unity negotiations started in June and July, 1958, after the failure of the April, 1958, general strike, and came to fruition in October and November, 1958.

Carlos Rafael Rodríguez also made some most revealing statements in 1958 to the French journalist, Claude Julien, about the relations of Castro and the Communists. According to Julien's book, *La Révolution Cubaine*, Carlos Rafael told Julien that he hoped the failure of the April, 1958, general strike would convince Castro of the necessity to include supporters of the former Presidents Prío and Grau San Martín in any future government and to subdue his anti-United States propaganda. Several weeks later, the Cuban poet Nicolás Guillén brought a letter, dated June 5, 1958, from Carlos

* A letter from Juan Marinello, then President of the Communist PSP, to Herbert Matthews, dated March 17, 1957, clearly states the Communist line before February, 1958. Marinello wrote: "In these days, and with reference to the assaults on barracks and expeditions from abroad—taking place without relying on popular support—our position is very clear; we are against these methods." Marinello went on to say that the 26th of July Movement had "noble aims" but followed "mistaken tactics," and "for that reason we do not approve of its actions" (Herbert L. Matthews, *The Cuban Story* [New York: George Braziller, 1961], pp. 51–52).

Rafael to Julien, who had returned to Paris. In this letter, Carlos Rafael revealed that the Communists did not think that "there already existed in the country the forces capable of overthrowing Batista and installing a progressive and anti-imperialist government in power." Therefore, he maintained, it was necessary to form "a coalition that would go beyond the limits of anti-imperialism, which necessarily includes forces that are not anti-imperialist," such as Prío Socarrás and Grau San Martín. In effect, the Communists at this date still considered Castro too weak and "extreme" to be able to overthrow Batista without an old-style "coalition."*

The timing of the Communist emissaries sent to make personal contact with Castro in the Sierra Maestra is also highly suggestive. Carlos Rafael Rodríguez made the trip in July, 1958, and Luis Más Martín the following month. The former, according to his own story, stayed for a while, went back to Havana for twenty days, and then returned to the Sierra for a longer stay, which lasted until Batista's downfall. Significantly, his second trip, probably in September, was made as official "representative of the Party," indicating that some agree-

* The French Communist journalist Georges Soria has written a book, *Cuba à l'heure Castro* (Paris: del Duca, 1961), which shows how secretive the Communists have become about their past relations with Castro. In 274 pages, Soria never so much as mentions the Cuban Communists in the struggle for power, and he alludes to them briefly for the first and only time on p. 269 merely to deny that the Cuban revolution was or had become a Communist one. Soria's monumental ignorance of Cuban politics and even of the story of his hero may be gathered from the fact that he makes the same basic mistake three times—asserting that Fidel Castro was an Auténtico in 1952–53. Castro was, of course, connected with the Ortodoxos, the most bitter enemies and rivals of the Auténticos. The equivalent mistake in U.S. politics would be not to know the difference between the Democrats and Republicans.

ment had been reached during his first visit and that he had gone back to Havana to get it approved by the top leadership (*Hoy*, January 11, 1959). Más Martín, a younger man who had been one of Fidel's friends in the university, was permitted to stay in the command post at La Plata, high up in the Sierra, where Castro himself directed operations (*Hoy*, January 15, 1959). Carlos Rafael was stationed at a headquarters on a lower level of the mountains at Las Vegas. The first Communist analysis after the victory indicates that the understanding was still somewhat informal and tentative. This "Thesis on the Present Situation" refers to a "coalition which is not a formal entity and does not correspond to precise accords between political organisms, but rather has arisen in action, in the defense of common objectives" (*Hoy*, January 11, 1959).

The inner history of Castro's regime remains to be told. Its main lines, however, have become increasingly clear. Fidel Castro—as much demagogue as idealist, as much adventurer as revolutionary, as much anarchist as Communist or anything else—was suddenly and unexpectedly catapulted into power without a real party, a real army, or a real program. In the struggle for power, he had put forward no original economic or political ideas and had stayed well within the limits of traditional democratic reform and idiom in Cuba. He differed from Batista's other enemies chiefly in the tactics he was willing to employ, in his faith in armed struggle and his willingness to organize it. But once power came into his hands, he refused to permit anything that might lessen or restrict it. He would not tolerate the functioning of a government that was not the façade of his personal rule or of a party that might develop a life of its own. His power and his promises were from the first incompatible, and this contradiction forced him to seek a basis for his regime wholly at variance with that of the anti-Batista revolution. He did not have the disciplined and experienced cadres, the ideology, and the international support to switch revolutions in full view of the audience. Only the Cuban and Russian Communists could make them available to him. Having formerly collaborated with Batista (whose government once contained both Juan Marinello and Carlos Rafael Rodríguez), the Cuban Communists were easily capable of collaborating with Castro. The "united front" of Communists and *Fidelistas* has been heading, as Guevara intimated in Moscow in December, 1960, toward a "united party," and if it materializes, Fidel Castro will certainly go down in history not as the *Líder Máximo* of a new movement but as the Pied Piper of an old one. Still, as long as the Communists need him at least as much as he needs them, further surprises cannot be ruled out; Fidel's ego may give the Communists as much trouble as it has given many others.

When I returned from Cuba in the spring of 1960, I wrote ("The Runaway Revolution," *The Reporter*, May 12, 1960): "Castro once spoke of his revolution as 'liberty with bread and without terror.' If he continues to push too hard, too fast, and too far, Cuba may yet have more terror without either bread or liberty." Unfortunately, my worst apprehensions have come true, and Fidel Castro has given Cuba not only a national revolution but an international civil war.

II. HOW *NOT* TO OVERTHROW CASTRO

The ill-fated invasion of Cuba in April, 1961, was one of those rare politico-military events—a perfect failure. So many things went wrong that it was relatively easy to fix the blame on anyone or anything connected with it. The organization responsible for the operation, the Central Intelligence Agency (CIA), came in for the largest share of criticism. But experience should warn us that the "intelligence failure" is usually the initial stage of a post-mortem. When a fiasco is really pure and complete, something deeper and more fundamental has probably been responsible. I do not think that the Cuban invasion is going to be an exception to the rule.

There were two sides to the failure, Cuban exile politics and United States policy. The first Cuban exiles to take refuge in the United States early in 1959 were the former *Batistianos*. Numbering only a few thousand, they succeeded mainly in giving Fidel Castro a propaganda point to score against the United States for harboring them. They were no serious threat to Castro's regime. They were thoroughly discredited, morally and politically. They were leaderless, since not even the most hardened and highly placed of dictator Fulgencio Batista's former henchmen dared to wish him back in power. They were, above all, utterly without support in Cuba itself.

Then came the frightened rich. Some of them were a step ahead of, or behind, Castro's newly formed Ministry for the Recovery of Illegally Acquired Property. Some simply preferred the rather less revolutionary atmosphere of Florida. Almost all had backed or belonged to parties of the Right, respectable or otherwise. Some had held their noses or had averted their eyes during the dictatorship, and a few had even contributed to Fidel's cause in the past.

The main exodus came the following year. It started in the spring, speeded up in the summer, and took on the proportions of a mass flight by the end of 1960. Among the spring refugees were the older politicians of the pre-Batista period, such as the former Premier, Manuel Antonio de Varona, and the former Minister of Education, Aureliano Sánchez Arango; some of them were urged on by the threat of physical violence, as in the case of Sánchez Arango. The large-scale expropriations that summer induced a great portion of the business community, big and small, to go. The purge of the universities and secondary schools drove out hundreds of teachers. The Communist takeover of the trade unions added many of their formerly pro-*Fidelista* officials to the stream. Professionals and intellectuals fled in increasingly large numbers. And, finally, Castro's own 26th of July Movement began to send a flow of disillusioned members and sympathizers to the United States, among them the former Minister of Public Works, Manuel Ray; the former Minister of Finance, Rufo López Fresquet; and the former President of the National Bank of Cuba, Felipe Pazos.

By 1961, over 100,000 political émigrés had gathered in the United States. And this number was only a fraction of those who had tried to get out but could not. If all who wanted to leave had been able to do so, the figure might easily have reached a quarter of a million, an incredible percentage for a small island with a total population of about 7 million. The emigration was top heavy with businessmen, professionals, and intellectuals, but skilled and semiskilled workers were conspicuous in the later stages of the outpouring. Nevertheless, the Cuban exiles were hardly representative of Cuban society as a whole.

Politically, the world of the exiles seemed like a crazy quilt. A staggering number and variety of *organizaciones*, *movimientos*, *asociaciones*, *comités*, *frentes*, *juntas*, *uniones*—and these categories do not exhaust the list—proliferated in Miami. The fragmentation, however, was less bizarre and alarming than it seemed because so many of the groups were little more than cliques of self-appointed leaders. In the profusion and confusion, three main tendencies could be distinguished—the traditional Right, Center, and Left—within which there were, of course, many different forms and shades.

In general, the Right had benefited from the old order in Cuba and was less opposed to it than disappointed that it had not lasted longer. It was passionately anti-Communist but cast its net so far and wide that some of President Kennedy's closest advisers could be—and, indeed, were—caught in it. The Center chiefly came out of the 1944–52 pre-Batista regimes of Ramón Grau San Martín and Carlos Prío Socarrás, with their peculiar mixture of promise and disappointment. Unlike the Right, its most responsible leaders had rejected and even conspired against Batista, but they had also rejected and in some cases had conspired against Castro as Batista's successor. The Left was mainly distinguished by its concern for social as well as political reform. It was drawn almost entirely from the former ranks of the 26th of July Movement, which, in the course of 1959, had split into pro- and anti-Communist segments.

Into this turmoil and strife among the thousands of desperate and impatient Cuban exiles, a catalyst injected itself, both of its own volition and by invitation.

INVASION IN THE WINGS

Former Vice President Richard M. Nixon has let it be known that he advocated training Cuban guerrilla forces to overthrow Castro as early as April, 1959. In that month, Castro and Nixon spent some time together in Washington, as a result of which Nixon wrote a three-page memorandum. Evidently he called Castro not a Communist but a "captive" of the Communists, and therefore even more dangerous. Since only the conclusions, but not the text, of Nixon's memorandum have been "leaked," it remains to be seen what Castro could have told Nixon to have justified such drastic action. Whatever it was, it was not enough to convince the other policy-makers, and American policy continued to be cautious and indecisive.

But what would have happened if Nixon's recommendation had been accepted? In the spring of 1959, the bulk of Cuban exiles in the United States were repentant or unrepentant *Batistianos*. The internal situation in Cuba was still fluid, whatever Fidel Castro's personal position may have been. The vast majority of Cubans as yet were admittedly under his spell. The Cuban Communists had already made great headway but they had run into resistance in Castro's own movement—as we now know, within his Cabinet—the full potential of which could not yet be determined. On his return to Cuba, in May, Castro found such dissension in his own ranks on the issue of Communism, and it was so openly expressed in the organ of the 26th of July Movement, *Revolución*, that he considered it necessary to make a major speech on May 8 in which he went to great pains to dissociate himself from "Communist ideas."

A Cuban guerrilla force in the spring or summer of 1959 would necessarily have been organized with the material at hand, and that material was almost exclusively composed of ex-Batista officers and soldiers. It would have been forced to invade a Cuba which was only beginning to show signs of disillusionment with Castro and which, in any case, still infinitely preferred—and perhaps always will prefer—him to Batista. And even if an invasion would have been "successful," it could have been only the first stage of a military occupation, wholly dependent on American arms, if not more, and faced with the hostility of the great majority of Cubans.

One can only marvel at this proposal of April, 1959. If Fidel Castro wanted the United States to do anything, it was to ally itself with the *Batistianos* in its midst. He had defeated them when they were in power, and he had least to fear from them when he was in power. In his eagerness to overthrow Castro, Nixon could think of nothing better than a military operation, and he was limited, whether he knew it or not, to the means at hand. His military "solution" was, in effect, political bankruptcy. It was rejected, and better judgment prevailed. Yet, a residue of Nixon's thinking remained, and it always hovered in the wings as an alternative policy if the situation continued to deteriorate.

Castro's propagandists have made a great deal of the fact that he was not invited by the American Government in April, 1959, and that no American offers of aid were made to him. The truth is, as several of his closest associates were aware, that Castro had made it known he did not want an official invitation and was not interested in offers of aid.* Whatever Castro may have said to

* Teresa Casuso, who was then a member of Castro's personal entourage, has written: "Our ambassador in Washington called me from that city to ask me if Fidel, now that he was going to the United States, wished an official invitation from the government, and if he should make a gesture in that direction. Fidel said no." Yet Señora Casuso thinks that Castro would have accepted an invitation if he had been offered one (*Cuba and Castro* [New York: Random House, 1961], p. 207). My own view is that Castro did not want an invitation, and the Eisenhower Administration was glad that he did not want one. The question of the offers of aid is discussed on pp. 157–60.

Nixon, his public statements, speeches, and interviews in the United States were among his most "democratic" utterances. After his departure, the Eisenhower Administration decided to send a new Ambassador to Havana, Philip W. Bonsal, with instructions of a conciliatory nature. But Castro would not see him for almost three months and then brushed him off publicly as a person of no importance.

POINT OF NO RETURN

The real point of no return in Cuba was passed in the fall of 1959, long before any overt American action was taken against the Castro regime. It was marked by the arrest of Hubert Matos, a schoolteacher by profession who had brought a planeload of arms and ammunition from Costa Rica to Castro's besieged forces in the Sierra Maestra mountains, in March, 1958. Matos fought through the rest of the rebellion, rose to the highest rank, major, and was entrusted after the victory with the military leadership of Camagüey Province. He was, therefore, in an exceptional position to know what was going on, and he began in the spring of 1959 to question why Communists were being put into leading positions in provincial and town administrations at the expense of 26th of July members.

When an epidemic of such replacements broke out in the rebel army itself, he decided to demonstrate his opposition. After vain efforts to discuss the matter with Castro, Matos' protest took the form of a resignation, which he sent on October 19. His case was not an individual aberration. A majority of the Camagüey army leaders, the head of the 26th of July Movement in the province, and others resigned with him. The scandal of the increasing Communist takeover in Camagüey was an open one, and opposition to it in the army and the movement had been building up for months.

Matos was arrested at home on October 20. Castro rushed to Camagüey and cracked down on the dissenters. The repercussions of this incident might have been less explosive in Castro's own top leadership if he had not insisted on charging Matos with "treason." The charge was too much for a group within the Cabinet, which had itself been watching with increasing misgivings the curious favoritism shown to Communists. One minister, Faustino Pérez, the former head of the Havana underground, refused to sign the Cabinet resolution denouncing Matos as a traitor. Toward the end of October, six Cabinet members came together for a private discussion —President Osvaldo Dorticós, Minister of Education Armando Hart, Minister of Public Works Manuel Ray, Minister of Transportation Julio Camacho, Minister of Communications Enrique Oltuski, and Faustino Pérez of the Ministry for the Recovery of Illegally Acquired Property. They agreed among themselves about the Communist danger, but one or two of them, probably Dorticós or Hart or both, reported the tenor of the discussion to Castro. He came to the Cabinet meeting the next day determined to force a showdown and insisted that anyone without full confidence in him did not belong in the Cabinet. Pérez and Ray expressed their views firmly. Oltuski and Hart spoke more ambiguously. Pérez had presented his resignation before the meeting and Ray did so afterward. Halfhearted efforts were made to change their minds, but they were permitted to go on November 26. At the same time, Major Ernesto (Che) Guevara replaced Dr. Felipe Pazos as head of Cuba's National Bank.

Matos' trial was held in December. I have read about ninety published pages of the record, including all of the most important testimony by Fidel Castro, and I suspect that the Matos trial will go down in recent Cuban history as the equivalent of the Moscow trials of the 1930's. Not a semblance of treason, in any meaningful sense of the term, was proved, or even charged, against Matos. He was merely accused of having been worried about the Communist advance, and it was contended that his resignation could have been so contagious that the regime might have been endangered. So it might have been, and so it is, in every system which provides no means for peaceful change and in which even the most passive forms of resistance take on a significance unthinkable in anything resembling a democratic order. Matos was condemned to twenty years' imprisonment. It contrasted oddly with the fifteen years—of which he had served only twenty months—to which Fidel Castro had been sentenced by the Batista dictatorship for leading a full-scale attack on an army barracks.*

The implications of Matos' punishment were boldly

* The partial record of the trial may be found in Pamphlet No. 3—". . . *y la luz se hizo*"—published by the Propaganda Secretariat of the Cuban Confederation of Labor. Matos' attorney, Francisco Lorie Bertot, has written three extremely revealing articles on the background and course of the trial itself ("Historia Interna del Proceso Hubert Matos," *Bohemia Libre*, January 14, 21, and 28, 1962).

exploited by the Communists. Early in February, 1960, Juan Marinello, President of the Communist PSP, for the first time publicly equated anti-Communism with treason: "He who raises the flag of anti-Communism raises the flag of the traitor." In the same month, Soviet Deputy Premier Anastas Mikoyan signed the first Soviet-Cuban agreement in Havana, amidst an official reception that betokened more than trade relations. In March, Blas Roca, the PSP's General Secretary, associated his party with the government and orientation of Fidel Castro, and offered the Communist program "to illuminate the road toward the historically inevitable transition to socialism."

Blas Roca's boasts provoked a reply from the popular writer and radio commentator Luis Conte Agüero, whose personal and political ties to Castro had been extremely close, but who now voiced the fear that the Communists were "achieving their purpose, pulling us instead of marching by our side." Immediately, Conte Agüero was crushed. The pro-Castro press attacked him so violently that he decided to go off the air. An organized crowd of demonstrators prevented him from making a farewell appearance. Castro himself devoted a four-hour television program to ridiculing, insulting, and denouncing him. Conte Agüero took the hint and sought refuge in a foreign embassy on his way out of the country.

These were episodes in what had become, for Fidel Castro, a second civil war. In the first, he had represented a democratic cause, and it had required a civil war against Batista's dictatorship. In the second, he represented a totalitarian alliance with the Communists, and it required a civil war against the democratic elements in his own movement. Castro waged the second civil war as ruthlessly as the first, striking down all those who stood in his way and leaving them only the alternatives of following him blindly or fighting back in a second underground.

FRD AND CIA

In the spring of 1960, the Eisenhower Administration made the decision which it had refused to make the previous spring and which led directly to the invasion attempt the following spring. For months, a strong if not the dominant wing of Cuban exiles had been seeking American support for every conceivable means of overthrowing Castro, including the arming and training of an invasion force. The exiles at this time were still predominantly representative of the Right, with little desire or ability to organize a democratic underground or to wean the masses of Cubans in Cuba away from Castro. After a year of resisting this pressure, the Administration, influenced by the course of events in Cuba, agreed to help organize a force of Cuban exiles—not necessarily to use it but to have it ready. The implementation of this decision, requiring the greatest secrecy, was entrusted to the Central Intelligence Agency. It need not be imagined that the Administration had to look for Cuban exiles to carry out its plan; plenty of exiles were perfectly satisfied with it and displeased only with the delay.

The first problem was which Cubans to work with. The initial choice fell on a group known as the Movimiento de Recuperación Revolucionario (MRR), of which the Secretary General was a former lieutenant of the rebel army in his late twenties—Manuel Artime. In the spectrum of Cuban exile politics at that time, the MRR stood somewhat left of center. It was, however, a relatively small group incapable of uniting the mass of exiles. To overcome this weakness, a united front was fostered, and the Frente Revolucionario Democrático (FRD) was formed by five groups early in June, 1960. The five groups were: Movimiento de Rescate Revolucionario, headed by Manuel Antonio de Varona; Movimiento Democrático Cristiano, of José Ignacio Rasco; Movimiento de Recuperación Revolucionario, of Manuel Artime; Asociación Montecristi, of Justo Carrillo; and the Frente Nacional Democrático (Triple A), of Aureliano Sánchez Arango. In effect, the FRD represented the Center of the exile world at a time when the Right was still unduly prominent and the Left had not yet arrived in large numbers. Since Artime was put in charge of the FRD's military activity, he remained the chief link to the CIA.

But the FRD also seemed unwieldy to the CIA. It was headed by a five-man Executive Committee, each with equal power, each jealous of his own status and distrustful of the others. The CIA made known that it preferred to deal with a single president or chairman of the Committee, and this demand precipitated a crisis in the FRD. One of its strongest personalities, Aureliano Sánchez Arango, had been complaining for some time about the very thing that outraged some of the Cuban leaders in the invasion attempt six months later—the treatment of the FRD as if it were an appendage of the CIA, subject to the latter's orders and incapable of living a life of its own. "The brief history of the relations between the FRD and the organism assigned to deal with Cuban questions is the history of an incessant series of pressures and impositions," were the first words in a confidential memorandum submitted by Sánchez Arango to the FRD on September 30, 1960. His protest went unheeded, and he took his organization out of the FRD.

But the other leaders of the FRD were satisfied with the arrangement, or at least not sufficiently dissatisfied to change it. "Tony" Varona was named "coordinator" of the remaining groups, and the FRD became more dependent than ever on the CIA. The first split in the FRD presents the Cuban-American problem in essence without any of the lurid details associated with the later invasion. Too many Cuban exile politicians of the Right and Center were content to accept the dictation of the CIA, just as the CIA was content to dictate to them.

For the amenable Cuban politicians, the arrangement was most convenient. At one stroke, they solved most of their financial and organizational problems outside the stresses and strains of the Cuban community. The best of these politicians were free of any taint of the Batista dictatorship, but their own pasts identified them with regimes that by their corruption had prepared the way for Batista, and they were hardly the symbols of a new Cuba determined to get something better than Batista or his predecessors.

On the American side, the Eisenhower Administration was, at best, cautious and indecisive; at worst, it played into Castro's hands. Such an administration was attracted, in time, to a military "solution" of the Cuban problem —tightly controlled from above, with a minimum commitment to any program that might disturb the sensibilities of the Cubans or the Americans who had benefited most from the *status quo ante*. For this purpose, the Eisenhower policy needed Cuban exiles who had not been compromised by the Batista or Castro regimes, but were not compromised by anything very different from the pre-Batista regimes either.

Yet the Eisenhower Administration was not capable of carrying out even this course consistently or successfully. The invasion force of Cuban exiles which the CIA undertook to organize did not reflect the political complexion of the FRD. Since the military operation was ostensibly a "nonpolitical" one, former members of Batista's army were readily admitted on the ground that their training and availability made them desirable. Most of them were, in fact, typical of the career officers and conscripts who had made up Batista's army, which had been in large part the pre-Batista army and had not fought very hard for him. But the sadists and "criminals" among them had enabled Castro to make the entire army a byword of shame and to disband it amidst a popular sigh of relief. Even on this unselective basis, moreover, the so-called invasion force did not amount to much. It numbered, I have been told, less than 1,000 until January, 1961. In effect, the Eisenhower Administration dawdled along without a serious political or military policy for a revolution that was plunging from stage to stage at breakneck speed.

ISSUES AND IMPLICATIONS

While this setup was able to withstand Sánchez Arango's walkout, it was threatened from another direction. By the summer of 1960, a different kind of Cuban exile began to arrive in the United States. José Miró Cardona, the Cuban Premier in the first six weeks of Castro's rule, sought asylum in July, and Manuel Ray, the former Minister of Public Works, went underground in May and left Cuba the following November. Except for his past association with the Castro regime, Miró Cardona was not noted for a radical social outlook, but Ray and others were unrepentant critics of Cuba's former political and social order. They were representative of that portion of the 26th of July Movement which had taken Castro's original program of democratic social reform seriously, had believed in him, and had reluctantly come to the realization that he was heading inexorably toward a form of Communist totalitarianism. They were not willing to repudiate all that had been done in Castro's first months in power, but neither were they willing to tolerate at any price the surrender of all political and intellectual freedom. They organized the Movimiento Revolucionario del Pueblo (MRP) and their first manifesto stated: "To fight against the '*Fidelismo-comunista*' faction is not to fight against the revolution for which thousands of Cubans gave their lives, but to redeem it from those who have betrayed it."

The influx of this group for the first time made the Left a serious rival of the Right and Center in the Cuban emigration. It did not take long for the other two wings to wake up to the threat and to launch a major political offensive against the newcomers. The issues may seem theoretical, but the implications were not.

Was the revolution betrayed? For the Right and a portion of the Center the answer was emphatically, No. They took the position that Fidel Castro and his closest aides had never been anything but, or anything better than, Communists, and that his revolution had always been Communist in character. They treated the 26th of July Movement as if it had been and still was a branch of or a cover for the official Communist Party. They condemned anyone who had ever belonged to the movement, and especially anyone who had occupied a post of some responsibility in Castro's government, as unfit for decent Cuban political intercourse.

It has seemed to me that the merest acquaintance with Castro's statements and promises before he took power demonstrates that he has used his power for altogether different ends. Like many arguments, however, this one may go on forever because the opposing sides tend to talk about different things. One side is really concerned with the inner intentions of Fidel Castro and his closest associates, especially his brother, Raúl, and his political mentor, Guevara. I would not rule out the possibility that Fidel always knew where he was going, and the likelihood is much greater for the other two. But from the available evidence, I strongly doubt it, at least in Fidel's case, and I am mildly amused that his enemies on the farthest Right should attribute to him a political consistency and integrity that he has done little to deserve. Whatever the answer to this question may prove to be, it will at most tell us something about Fidel, not about his entire movement.

For the 26th of July Movement was never homogeneous, and the larger it grew in 1957 and 1958, the less homogeneous it became. It included those who merely wished to restore the Constitution of 1940 and those who demanded "a real social revolution." It attracted those who admired and those who detested the United States. It took in fervent anti-Communists and ardent fellow-travelers. To hold this conglomeration together, Castro had progressively moderated his program and propaganda. By 1958, he had voiced little more than the traditional aspirations of the socially conscious, democratic-minded Cuban middle and working classes. He may not have been sincere, but many of those who followed him undoubtedly were.

Those who insist that Castro has led a Communist revolution from the start have never thought through the implications of their position. The overwhelming majority of Cubans of all classes were admittedly pro-Castro in January, 1959. If they wittingly supported a Communist revolution and knowingly preferred a Communist regime, the anti-Communist cause in Cuba was lost at the outset. But no one, least of all Fidel Castro, has even intimated that this was the case. He took special pains in the first months of his regime to assure the Cuban people that he was not a Communist; the organ of the 26th of July Movement conducted a war of words with the organ of the official Communist Party; and the anti-Communists in his Cabinet made no secret of their views. All this may have been a blind, but it was a blind made necessary by the non-Communist character of the revolution. Whatever may have been Castro's personal intent, it should not be confused with the entire anti-Batista rebellion, which was much larger and broader than even the 26th of July Movement.

Nevertheless, Castro's ex-associates in exile were met with a furious campaign which accused them of something called "*Fidelismo sin Fidel.*" It is not clear how *Fidelismo* can exist without Fidel, since he has always been the essential charismatic ingredient that made it possible. And it is not clear what *Fidelismo* is, since it has been several different things in its relatively brief life. In its public expression, the *Fidelismo* of 1958 was only distantly related to the *Fidelismo* of 1960, and even less to the *Fidelismo* of 1961 or 1962. But whatever "*Fidelismo sin Fidel*" may mean, it served to make the break with Castro's regime by Ray, Pazos, and the rest of the MRP seem superficial and untrustworthy. If *Fidelismo* was just the same or just as bad as Communism, it made them seem just the same or just as bad as Communists, with or without faith in Fidel. And yet, paradoxically, they had broken with Fidel precisely because they had believed him when he used to say that *Fidelismo* and Communism were intrinsically different, and because they had refused to follow him into Communism.

These controversies were not altogether theoretical. They were intimately related to a practical question of crucial importance—whether the underground in Cuba or the exiles in the United States should constitute the primary front in the struggle against Castro. For some, the underground came first, and the role of the exiles was mainly to assist and support it. For others, the exiles came first, and the underground had virtually no place in their plans. This choice between the underground and the exiles was one of the chief dividing lines between the Left and the Right. The Left invariably stressed the underground, the Right was almost exclusively in favor of the exiles, and there were elements of the Center in both camps. Those with an underground orientation could not hope to be effective in Cuba with the same type of program and propaganda that might appeal to many exiles in the United States. The underground had to live and work among Cubans who in the great majority had once believed in Castro and who were most likely to turn against him because he had disappointed them. Many of the exiles had never had any faith in Castro to lose, and he was just as obnoxious to them before taking power as after.

Thus the war against Castro was inextricably bound up with the war among the exiles, and theoretical issues were inextricably bound up with practical implications. A debate over the "revolution betrayed" was also a dispute over the overthrow of Castro primarily by forces in Cuba or by forces in the United States. A decision to organize a relatively small, tightly controlled, professionally led invasion force was an expression both of American policy and of Cuban exile politics. And, in a deeper sense, the future was at stake, too. The original aims of the 26th of July Movement had been so far removed from Communism that Castro had been forced to betray or falsify them in order to go from one to the other. Yet these aims had once united the overwhelming majority of the Cuban people, and they could conceivably rise again in one form or another as the historic aspirations of the people as a whole. After all, there had been almost nothing in the program of the 26th of July Movement that had been original with Fidel Castro, and the basic Cuban problems it reflected were bound to exist with or without him. Thus, the cry that went up against "*Fidelismo sin Fidel*" was intended to foreclose the future of Cuba to any such radical democratic revolution as *Fidelismo* had once represented.

THE FUSION

Meanwhile, in Cuba itself another turning point was reached. I have already suggested that a decisive step was taken in the fall of 1959 with the arrest of Hubert Matos in October; the replacement of Ray, Pérez, and Pazos, and the first stage of the Communist takeover of the Cuban Confederation of Labor, in November; and the cruel punishment of Matos in December. American policy played a relatively minor role in this period. The crisis came from within Castro's own 26th of July Movement and had been brewing from his first month in power. It was generated not by the United States but by the Communists, or rather by their sponsors and protectors in the Cuban Government.

The next major step came in the summer of 1960. Although it was far more closely related to actions taken by the United States, and has received much more publicity, it was but another stage in a continuous process rather than an impulsive, unpremeditated beginning.

The final rupture between Cuba and the United States was precipitated in June, 1960, by the Cuban demand that three U.S.- and British-owned oil refineries in Cuba process two bargeloads of Soviet crude oil. The companies refused, and their refineries were quickly taken over. In July, after hesitating for months, the Eisenhower Administration suspended the 700,000 tons that remained of Cuba's total 1960 sugar quota of about 3 million tons. Cuba retaliated with a decree expropriating all enterprises and properties wholly or partially owned by U.S. citizens or companies. Most of this expropriation was carried out in August, the rest in September.

These events cannot be understood by themselves, and the "cause" of the wholesale expropriation of American property was only superficially the oil and sugar disputes. The Cuban Government had not been paying the three companies for over two years and had piled up a huge debt of $16 million for oil imports and $60 million for previous refining. The companies had given up hope of ever getting their money back and expected to be taken over anyway. The Cuban case was based on the Mineral Fuel Law of 1938, which required foreign-owned refineries to process Cuban crude petroleum. The companies replied that this law referred only to oil taken from Cuban soil. Indeed, the oil companies accounted for only a small portion of the U.S. credits extended to the Castro regime, the total of which amounted to over $200 million.

As for the sugar quota, the Cuban attitude had been stated by the clairvoyant Guevara early in March, 1960: "There is some talk about lowering the Cuban sugar quota, indeed, of suspending it altogether. The sooner the better. For Cuba, it is a symbol of colonialism. We shall be better off without imperialist yokes." After that, it was a tussle between the Castro regime and the Eisenhower Administration to see which could maneuver the other into providing the best alibi and bearing the most blame for lowering or suspending the quota. I doubt that the Eisenhower Administration came off best in this contest, but I am also skeptical that more adroit tactics would have changed anything fundamentally.

Moreover, Castro's wave of expropriation did not stop with American-owned companies. On October 13, 1960, at one blow, Law No. 890 nationalized 376 all-Cuban enterprises, including 18 distilleries, 5 breweries, 4 paint factories, 61 textile factories, 16 rice mills, 11 movie theaters, and 13 department stores. Some, as in the case of the well-known Bacardí company, had supported Castro against Batista. The Castro regime expropriated over 3 million acres of U.S.-owned land, but soon afterward also expropriated almost as much Cuban-owned land. The expropriation of foreign properties was clearly only a part of a much larger transformation, and the latter cannot be accounted for by the refusal of three oil companies to refine some Soviet oil, or the suspension of 700,000 tons of the sugar quota, the total elimination of which none other than Guevara had demanded, "the sooner the better."

Nationalization had never been in Castro's program, except for the electric and telephone companies, and by 1958, he had even changed his mind, or at least said he had, about them. In the fall of 1960, he nationalized on a scale that had appeared inconceivable that very spring. No one reading the Cuban press or speaking to anyone in the regime could have anticipated it. If this was the transition from the "bourgeois-democratic" to the "proletarian" stage of the revolution, the Cuban proletariat had little or nothing to do with it. The Castro movement had never considered itself socialist, and had never, therefore, advocated socialism or conducted any socialist education. Nor had the official Communists been demanding nationalization or intimating that the time had come for socialism in Cuba. The Cuban trade unions were certainly not the repositories of socialist faith. First came "socialism," and then the proletariat was told how lucky it was to have it.

Such transition as there was took place wholly in the top leadership of Castro's regime. The bellwether, as always, was Guevara. At the end of July, 1960, he informed a youth congress in Havana that the Cuban revolution was "Marxist." He reiterated this thought in an article in *Verde Olivo*, in October. Then, on November 7, at a celebration in Havana of the Bolshevik Revolution, a trade-union leader, José María de la Aguilera, ventured that it was time to say without fear "that we are marching inexorably toward socialism in our country." These brief and isolated statements exhaust the published references to "Marxism" or "socialism" in 1960. They indicate that something was going on in the top echelons of the Castro leadership, but as usual, Fidel Castro himself waited for the right occasion before committing himself—a very different matter from the naïve notion that the occasion caused him to commit himself.

The summer of 1960 also introduced a new stage in Soviet-Cuban relations. In July, Soviet Premier Nikita Khrushchev threatened to retaliate with Soviet rockets if Cuba were attacked, a commitment he later qualified as "really symbolic." By the end of the month, Fidel Castro announced the arrival of the first automatic rifles from Czechoslovakia. By November 8, he exulted: "We have acquired arms, much arms, much more of them than the mercenaries and the imperialists have imagined." Guevara made another long pilgrimage to the East in October–December, 1960, and on his return explained, with his usual brutal candor, what had motivated the Soviet bloc to sign up for large quantities of Cuban sugar. The Soviets produced so much sugar themselves that they did not need any from Cuba, he said, but they were willing to give the Cubans advantageous terms for "political" reasons (*Obra Revolucionaria*, 1961, No. 2).

And economic aid was not the only thing the Soviets were willing to give for "political" considerations. At a parade in Havana on January 2, 1961, the full range of arms shipments from the Soviet bloc was put on display —heavy tanks, 55-mm. and 105-mm. cannon, truck-drawn field artillery, mortars, rocket launchers, anti-aircraft guns, antitank guns, and automatic weapons. On March 4, Castro declared that "Cuba can obtain mountains on mountains of Communist arms," and "Cuba now has more thousands of tons of arms than a year ago." These weapons, and the training that went with them, had obviously resulted from more "political" agreements reached many months before.

The "politics" of the trade agreements and arms shipments was internal as well as external. This aspect of the new situation can also be traced back to the summer of 1960. In August, 1960, at the Eighth Congress of the PSP, General Secretary Blas Roca set forth the perspective of "complete union," or "fusion," of all the revolutionary forces "in a single movement." At the end of October, as the first installment of fusion, the youth divisions of the PSP and the 26th of July Movement merged to form the Asociación de Jóvenes Rebeldes (Association of Young Rebels). In December, at the meeting of the Communist Parties in Moscow, Guevara mentioned the prospect of a "united party" in Cuba.

To help the merger along, Blas Roca and Fidel Castro said *mea culpa* to atone for their old sins against each other. The Communists had to live down their former contempt for Castro's assault on the Moncada Barracks in 1953 as a "petty-bourgeois putsch." At the Eighth Congress, Blas Roca made amends by giving Fidel credit for seeing the possibilities of, and taking the practical steps toward, armed struggle to overthrow the Batista dictatorship.

Fidel had a similar problem. Once upon a time—on May 21, 1959, to be exact—he had distinguished his revolution from capitalism and Communism, the one because it "killed people with hunger," the other because it suppressed their liberties, "the liberties which are so dear to man." The human being, he had proclaimed, was being sacrificed in both the capitalist and Communist states, and Cuba intended to make its own "autochthonous" revolution, as distinctive as its music. These words, and others like them, were characteristic of his first months in power; a proud and even arrogant Castro used to insist that the Cuban revolution had its own superior ideology. For the Communists, the memory rankled, and something had to be done before a "complete union" could be sanctified.

On February 1, 1961, the Italian Communist organ, *L'Unità*, published an interview with Castro of unusual significance. One of the questions asked by its correspondent in Havana, Arminio Savioli, was: "Major, what is your opinion of the Partido Socialista Popular, the party of the Cuban Communists?"

Castro replied:

> It is the only Cuban party that has always clearly proclaimed the necessity for a radical change of structure, of social relationships. It is also true that at first the Communists distrusted me and us rebels. It was a justified distrust, an absolutely correct position, ideologically and politically. The Communists were right to be distrustful because we of the Sierra, leaders of the guerrillas, were still full of petty-bourgeois prejudices and defects, despite Marxist reading. The ideas were not clear to us, though we wanted with all our strength to destroy tyranny and privileges. Then we came together, we understood each other, and began to collaborate. The Communists have given much blood, much heroism, to the Cuban cause. Now we continue to work together, loyally and fraternally.

This new note of ideological inferiority was struck again in a carefully prepared speech by Castro on March 25. The occasion was also typical of the new era. The International Organization of Journalists, a Communist group with headquarters in Prague, had awarded its annual prize to *Revolución*, the organ of the 26th of July Movement, or what remains of it. In celebration of the event, *Hoy*, the official Cuban Communist newspaper, sponsored a banquet for more than 2,000 people in honor of *Revolución* at which the Premier was the main speaker. One passage harked back to the past in the same curiously apologetic and even guilty way.

> The revolution was beginning. It was a process that had to go on for a long time; it had to go on step by step. It was weak in its origins; it was above all weak in the ideological sphere. The leaders of the revolution had great support among the people, the revolution in itself had an extraordinary amount of sympathy, for what it had cleared away, not for what it had done; but, ideologically, the revolution was weak.

And, in a public address in Havana on March 13, in the presence of Premier Castro, the Cuban Ambassador to the Soviet Union, Faure Chomón, employed the expression "we Communists."

There was always only one real party in Castro's Cuba, the Communist PSP, but it was not good form to show too much deference or attribute too much prominence to it publicly. All that changed by the summer of 1960. The old-time Communist leaders, Blas Roca, Juan Marinello, Carlos Rafael Rodríguez, Aníbal Escalante, Lázaro Peña, and the rest—all products of the school of Stalinism for a quarter of a century—formerly content to work in the background, stepped forward to claim their due. The members of the PSP's Buró Ejectivo, or

Politburo, became busy addressing a new type of audience—of government employees.* The former Communist head of the Cuban Confederation of Labor, Lázaro Peña, again visibly emerged as the strong man of its top leadership.† *Verde Olivo* was always considered the most openly Communist of the official government organs, but now the popular magazine *Bohemia* began to run it a close second. A feature article on Juan Marinello referred to him and Blas Roca as "pupils of the greatest university of all: the marvelous university of Marxism-Leninism" (*Bohemia,* March 26, 1961).

One more sign of the times in Cuba was the fate of a book. The well-known bookshop in Havana Librería Venecia had ordered copies of Boris Pasternak's *Doctor Zhivago* in a Spanish translation published in Buenos Aires. The books arrived, but the owner of the shop, Ricardo del Campo Gordón, received a notice that they had been seized as counterrevolutionary literature. He no longer runs a bookshop in Cuba. Recent visitors have been impressed by the place of honor given to the works of Lenin, Stalin, Mao Tse-tung, and Khrushchev

* *Revolución,* March 24, 1961, for example, devoted a column and a half to a talk on economic planning by Carlos Rafael Rodríguez to the officials and employees of the National Institute of Sports, Physical Education, and Recreation, at which its Director General presided. Another column and a half reported a lecture by Aníbal Escalante, Executive Secretary of the PSP, on "The Cuban Revolution, Its Character and Its Development" to employees and officials of the Ministry of Finance.

† *Bohemia* (Havana), March 26, 1961, carried an article on the CTC, accompanied by photographs of six leaders. The picture of Lázaro Peña led all the rest. At the 1961 May Day parade in Havana, he marched in the first line, next to Minister of Industries Guevara, President Dorticós, Premier Castro, and Blas Roca, in that order. (The owner and editors of the original *Bohemia* went into exile and now publish *Bohemia Libre* in New York and Caracas.)

in the bookshop of the government-owned Imprenta Nacional in the lobby of the hotel Habana Libre (formerly the Havana Hilton).*

A major change in agricultural policy was also introduced. Hitherto, the so-called cooperatives had received the most attention and publicity. By the beginning of 1961, however, it became clear that the "cooperatives" were devoted mainly to sugar production and that the cattle industry had been reserved for a different type of agricultural organization—*Granjas del Pueblo* (People's Farms), modeled on the Soviets' *sovkhoz* (state-farm) system. A report on May 17, 1961, by Captain Antonio Núñez Jiménez, Executive Director of the Agrarian Reform Institute (INRA), revealed that the cooperatives had taken second place to the *granjas* in area; the *granjas* already covered 6,567,426 acres, or 29.16 per cent of all productive land, and the cooperatives only 2,664,000 acres, 11.83 per cent of the productive land. The cooperatives were still ahead in manpower, 122,448 to 96,498, but at the present rate of growth, the *granjas* may soon forge ahead in this respect, too. In any event, the cooperatives are so tightly controlled by INRA that they could and probably will be easily transformed into *granjas* whenever the Castro regime pleases to go all the way.

Outside Cuba, rumors of a deal between Castro and his archenemy, Generalissimo Rafael Leónidas Trujillo, of the Dominican Republic, began to spread late in 1960. One Dominican radio station suddenly started

* Fritz René Allemann, "Die Revolution der Bärtigen," *Der Monat*, April, 1961.

to specialize in pro-Castro and anti-United States propaganda. Then, in a speech on January 6, 1961, Guevara referred to Trujillo as "now our friend" (*Obra Revolucionaria*, 1961, No. 2). That this remark was not entirely ironic was subsequently demonstrated by Raúl Castro. In a speech on June 4, 1961, Raúl developed the idea that Trujillo had been useful to imperialism for three decades but that the Dominican dictator had lost his usefulness and had become an "obstacle." Therefore, Raúl suggested, the United States had decided to get rid of Trujillo, and Trujillo had "suspended the attacks against Cuba." Whereas Trujillo had previously been characterized as a bloody tyrant, Raúl now paid tribute to him as "a daring and audacious type, personally even brave." Traditionally, in Communist policy, a deal can be made with a Hitler or a Trujillo once he is defined "objectively" as an "obstacle" to imperialism; there was probably some practical reason why Raúl went to so much trouble to explain that Trujillo had become such an "obstacle" and thereby to imply that Castro and Trujillo faced the same enemy.

Raúl was also the author of the most important article published in Cuba on the eighth anniversary of the attack on the Moncada Barracks, in 1953. He chose to publish this article in the June–July, 1961, issue of *Fundamentos*, the official monthly organ of the Communist PSP. Only PSP members had ever before been permitted to write for *Fundamentos*, and this article strongly hinted that Raúl's ties to the PSP were much closer than had ever been admitted. It suggested not only that fusion had already become an accomplished fact in all but name but also the probability that Raúl's "fusion" with the Communists had taken the form of membership in the PSP some time before, perhaps long before.*

And having been named one of the 1961 winners of the Lenin Peace Prize, Fidel made a speech on May 19 in which he showed how far he had traveled politically by bursting out: "Glory to our great José Martí! Glory to our great Vladimir Ilich Ulyanov, Lenin!"

One reason for these developments was suggested by Castro himself in his interview in *L'Unità*. He was asked: "What has the Socialist camp contributed to the Cuban revolution?" To which he replied: "My boy, what would have happened to us if Khrushchev had not sent us oil, if he had not bought our sugar? And if the Czechoslovaks had not sent us the arms to defend ourselves? And machines, spare parts, technicians?"

The economic agreements, the arms shipments, and the piecemeal political fusion were not separate, unrelated events; they were interconnected aspects of a single, simultaneous process. Of the three, the last undoubtedly signified the most. As long as Castro maintained even a nominal political independence in Cuba, his foreign relations might be distinguished from his internal political position. This distinction had been fading to the vanishing point. Whatever the nascent "united party" might

* Raúl's ties with the Communists may go back to 1952–53. In this very article, he remarks that some members of the Ortodoxo youth movement joined the Communist youth after Batista's coup in 1952, and he may very well know because he was one of them (p. 9). In any case, he was so much the Communists' favorite by the time Batista fell that in the very first issue of *Hoy*, dated January 6, 1959, more than one full page was devoted to reprinting an interview with Raúl and another half-page to a report of his unit's exploits—out of a total of four pages!

be called, it would merely be an enlarged version of the official Communist Party. It would, in effect, represent the induction of the top-ranking *Fidelistas* into the PSP.

I cannot suppress the feeling that the new self-critical Fidel is totally out of character. Whatever might be the reasons for submitting to the ideology of the Party, he could hardly transfer his *mystique* to it, and it still needed him at least as much as he needed it. Yet Castro's newborn humility before the Communists was not merely a pose. He enjoyed the greatest advantage over them in the years of struggling for power, less and less after winning power. While they were still advocating "clean, democratic elections" to get rid of Batista,* he celebrated force and force alone. But in that period, his political program betrayed little originality; it was, if anything, less radical than that put forward by Grau San Martín in 1933. Since Castro took power without a real ideology, a real army, or a real party, he could conceivably have survived without them only by making his power consistent with his promises, and thus holding his original backing together. But this is precisely what he chose not to do.

In the Communist-style state that he established in Cuba in less time than it took the Bolsheviks in Soviet Russia, a new ideology, a new army, and a new party were urgently needed. For all his old boasts that the Cuban revolution was unlike any other and needed no ideology, army, or party, Castro turned to all three for

* Declaration of the National Committee, signed by Marinello and Blas Roca, June 28, 1958.

survival, and they are not at all the seemingly fresh, innocent experiments that so enamored sympathetic observers in the past.

Fidel Castro must certainly be ranked with the greatest mass intoxicators of the century, but no one is likely to mistake him for a creative political thinker. For a long time, he was dependent on the superior intellect of Guevara, who, unlike his nominal chieftain, never wastes words and should always be taken seriously. Guevara once told Mme. Simone de Beauvoir that he would "spend hours explaining a complex economic problem to Fidel," who would then successfully boil it down to half an hour on television the next day. This is the inestimable gift of the popularizer and demagogue, not the genius of an original social revolutionary, and both Castro's strength and weakness explain his usefulness and subservience to the Communists.

SIGNS OF CHANGE

In the summer and fall of 1960, while great changes were taking place in Cuba, the United States was preoccupied with the election campaign and change of administrations. The new Administration was far from a free agent, as a result of the extreme anti-Castro position assumed by John F. Kennedy in the campaign and of the actions taken by his predecessor, especially the rupture of diplomatic relations, in January, 1961. Nevertheless, a re-examination of United States policy vis-à-vis Cuba was undertaken.

On one level, changes occurred. The most notable, on

the Cuban exile side, was the formation, in March, 1961, of the Cuban Revolutionary Council, headed by Dr. José Miró Cardona. While the former American policy had favored the Centrist FRD, the new Revolutionary Council was based on both the FRD and MRP, a distinct shift to the left. The Council's Declaration of April 9, 1961, clearly reflected this political shift. "We are not, nor could we be, counterrevolutionaries," it asserted. "We were revolutionists who fought against the previous regime, which had impoverished the whole country for the benefit of a minority lusting for gold and power. It is with the same convictions that we now oppose the present regime, which has betrayed our country and plunged it into chaos."

Another passage stated: "Let there be no mistake. During the immediate post-revolutionary period some ideals of the people, which were a part of the national goal, were achieved. It will be necessary to incorporate them into the provisions of the Constitution. There will be no going back to a past which we all oppose—neither Communism nor reaction."*

The second evidence of a change was the so-called White Paper on Cuba issued by the State Department. This document defined the "grave and urgent challenge" of Castro's Cuba as follows: "The challenge results from the fact that the leaders of the revolutionary regime betrayed their own revolution, delivered that revolution into the hands of powers alien to the hemisphere, and transformed it into an instrument employed with calcu-

* The full text in English was published in *The New York Times*, April 9, 1961.

lated effect to suppress the rekindled hopes of the Cuban people for democracy and to intervene in the internal affairs of other American Republics."

The U.S. document also interpreted the "betrayal" in the same sense as the Declaration of the Revolutionary Council: "The positive programs initiated in the first months of the Castro regime—the schools built, the medical clinics established, the new housing, the early projects of land reform, the opening up of beaches and resorts to the people, the elimination of graft in government—were impressive in their conception; no future Cuban government can expect to turn its back on such objectives. But so far as the expressed political aims of the revolution were concerned, the record of the Castro regime has been a record of the steady and consistent betrayal of Dr. Castro's pre-revolutionary promises; and the result has been to corrupt the social achievements and make them the means, not of liberation, but of bondage."

On paper, the line had clearly veered to the left. The change was taken seriously not only by the Left-wing MRP but by the Right-wing Cuban exiles who immediately stepped up their campaign against the "revolution betrayed" and "*Fidelismo sin Fidel.*" The organ of the extreme Right, *Diario de la Marina*, went into paroxysms of rage and vituperation not only against the ex-*Fidelistas* but against the "leftists in the State Deparment" and "the SOCIALISTS in Washington."* All those groups that had been left out of, or would not come into, the Revolutionary Council, many of them on the right, met to-

* *Diario de la Marina* (Miami Beach), March 18, 1961. Also see the next three issues for more of the same.

gether at the end of March, 1961, and formed a Junta Revolucionaria de Liberación Nacional, with Aureliano Sánchez Arango as Secretary General.

The practical implications of the Declaration of the Revolutionary Council and the White Paper of the State Department were, indeed, incompatible with the Right-wing policy of a small, professionally trained, tightly controlled invasion force to "liberate" Cuba from the outside. As late as January, 1961, Dr. Miró Cardona, after predicting that a "general uprising" was fast approaching, was asked: "But is that enough? Will there have to be an invasion?" To which he replied: "After the uprising, there will have to be a military decision on whether to help the people with a mass invasion or with a continuation of the infiltration by specially trained men. It is impossible at this point to decide whether a mass invasion will be necessary."* This emphasis on the internal uprising as the primary front in the anti-Castro struggle was a fundamental tenet of the Left.

But what to do with the relatively small, professionally trained, tightly controlled invasion force that had been inherited from the Eisenhower Administration? In January, 1961, recruiting started once more and about 500 more men were added, for a total of less than 1,500. Again, little political differentiation was made in the selection of recruits. This very lack of discrimination, however, was indirectly responsible for influencing the political composition of the force. Many former members and even officers of the rebel army were available in the emigration. But most of them would not fight

* *U.S. News & World Report,* January 23, 1961.

alongside former members of Batista's army and police, and certainly would not serve under them. I have been told that the ex-*Batistianos* made up only about 15 per cent of the total but that their percentage went up sharply in the leadership. In one Guatemalan camp with about 300 men, it was reported, one ex-*Batistiano* officer was enough to cause 230 of them to go on strike. Nevertheless, the invasion force was broadly representative of the entire exile community—from *Batistianos* to the sons of Varona and Miró Cardona, from professional military cadres to idealistic young professionals.

BEHIND THE INVASION

The preparation for an "invasion" of Cuba was divulged in the Guatemalan paper *La Hora* as early as October 30, 1960, and it was then described as "well under way." The alarm about the Guatemalan camps was first raised in the United States by a most unlikely source—the Director and staff of the *Hispanic American Report*, published by the Institute of Hispanic American and Luso-Brazilian Studies at Stanford University. After some hesitation, the U.S. press went after the story and succeeded in making the camps an open secret without being able to dig out some of the vital details. Some of the figures, guessed at or planted, were ludicrously inflated, and they later contributed to the public misconception of the entire operation.

But the Cuban exile leaders had been wrestling with their consciences about the relatively small force in the camps for a long time, and they knew how politically explosive it was. Before the negotiations for the Revolutionary Council could be consummated, a hitherto unpublished agreement was reached between the Frente Revolucionario Democrático and the Movimiento Revolucionario del Pueblo:

CONFIDENTIAL BASES OF UNITY BETWEEN THE "FRENTE REVOLUCIONARIO DEMOCRÁTICO" AND THE "MOVIMIENTO REVOLUCIONARIO DEL PUEBLO"*

I. FUNDAMENTAL ORGANIZATION OF THE PROVISIONAL GOVERNMENT

1. The person designated to preside over the Revolutionary Council will select freely the members of the Council indispensable for the tasks in exile; the others will be selected in Cuba, inasmuch as the Revolutionary Council should be formed by persons in exile but also, in its majority, by persons fighting in Cuba when the [present] regime falls and who, for reasons of security, cannot be designated now.

2. Once the Communist tyranny collapses, the Council of Ministers of the Provisional Government will be formed by members with portfolio to carry out the exclusive function of government and by six to ten members without portfolio who, jointly with the members with portfolio, will exercise the legislative function.

3. These members without portfolio will be designated by the President of the Revolutionary Council, who will select them from lists of three names submitted by each revolutionary group.

* Unofficial translation.

4. This Revolutionary Council will assume the functions of the Provisional Government when it moves to Cuba.

II. INSURRECTIONAL STRUGGLE

1. The Council that is formed as a consequence of this agreement must give maximum priority to the aid of the combatants who are already inside Cuba fighting against the Communist oppressor.

2. No person who held an objectionably responsible position with the criminal dictatorship of Batista can be admitted into any armed force that may be organized outside of Cuba. Because of the very harmful effect that any apparent utilization of these elements can have, both organizations agree that they must share the responsibilities of preventing even the use of these persons in the recruiting offices.

3. The military commands of all the revolutionary forces that may be organized outside of Cuba must be in the hands of Cubans who give full guarantee to the President of the Council and to both groups (that sign this document) with respect to their integrity and understanding, their responsibilities and functions in a democratic society, their full deference to the authority of the Revolutionary Council during the insurrectional struggle and to the Civil Government of the Republic.

4. The Revolutionary Council must immediately assume the responsibility that these criteria should fully prevail in the forces which are being organized.

III. AGRARIAN REFORM

Both groups declare that they will take steps to reach an agreement within the next two weeks on the effective form of prohibiting *latifundia*, as a consequence of which a fundamental criterion would be established to avoid harmful conflicts at the initiation of the Provisional Government.

New York, March 22, 1961

For the FRD	*For the MRP*
A. de Varona	M. Ray

The second section of this document clearly embodied a point of view that made the underground in Cuba the primary front and sought to remove any possible taint of *Batistismo* from the invasion force organized outside of Cuba. In principle, there was no reason why Castro should not have been opposed by forces inside and outside Cuba, as Batista had been opposed. But the two forms of opposition could work against each other as well as with each other. Priority to the outside force could have a negative effect on the underground, which might be encouraged to wait for "liberation" from the outside. The inclusion of *Batistianos* in the invasion force would not sit as well with the Cubans in Cuba as with some of those in exile. And the political orientation necessary for the underground struggle differed drastically from the political outlook, or lack of it, characteristic of the invasion force.

The Revolutionary Council and the White Paper represented one side of the new Kennedy Administration's policy, the invasion force the other side, and never the twain did meet. In the twelve days that elapsed between the "Confidential Bases," signed by Varona and

Ray, and the decision to send the invading force to Cuba, nothing had changed, and in so short a time, nothing could have changed. A real change of policy would have required a sharply reversed attitude toward the underground and a complete overhauling of the invasion force. But time was the one thing that could not be reversed or overhauled. A few more months of the Soviet bloc's "mountains on mountains" of arms to Cuba made any new, long-range plan appear to be increasingly difficult and dangerous. Many of the Cuban exiles had been gripped by what may be called a "deadline fixation." They were persuaded, and bent on persuading everyone else, that if Castro were not overthrown by March or April—or June, at the latest—he could never be overthrown.*

This frantic desperation that time was running out, combined with an intense conviction that there would never be a better time, was apparently contagious. The notion that the United States gathered together a few "mercenaries" for the invasion ludicrously misses the point. The Cuban exiles themselves exerted a tremendous pressure for quick action, and their only apprehension was of the lengths to which the United States might go to help them. In the training camps, a similar mood prevailed, and the option seemed to be to use the force,

* This "deadline" thinking was later reflected by the then Director of the CIA, Allen W. Dulles, who said that "I think the historians of the future will probably say that if any move was to be made to get rid of Communism in Cuba short of actual military intervention with all the power of the United States, that effort would probably have to have been made sometime between, say, November [1960] and April [1961]" ("Meet the Press" television program, December 31, 1961).

such as it was, or to disband it. In effect, without starting over again, the Kennedy Administration was basically limited to the policies and instrumentalities of the Eisenhower Administration.

In the end, the Cuban Revolutionary Council served as a fig leaf for the invasion. Maximum priority was given to the outside invasion force, not to the Cuban underground. Objectionable personnel were admitted and not weeded out of the invasion force. The Council was not in command of the situation, and its members were humiliated by those who were.

On the surface, two different lines were pursued simultaneously, one for the Revolutionary Council, another for the invasion force. The former implied that some re-examination had taken place in the Kennedy Administration; the latter amounted to an expression of modified Nixonism. The difference between these two lines is the key to what was wrong with the conception, as well as the execution, of this invasion.

The invasion force was given such absolute priority that the anti-Castro forces inside Cuba were virtually ignored. The inversion of the two was a crucial factor. By putting the invasion first, the Intelligence Agency could only guess at how far the popular rebellion against Castro had gone or what it was capable of doing. It was apparent, even from the speeches that Castro and Guevara had been making, that the Castro regime had been slipping in popular support for months, especially in the middle and working classes. But the opposition knew that it had made the least headway among the peasantry, the teenagers, a portion of those whose existence was wholly dependent on the all-embracing state machine, an indeterminate propaganda-drenched group in all classes, and, of course, the committed Communists and hero-worshiping *Fidelistas*. The process of disenchantment could not be forced artificially, and in the nature of a repressive state, even those closest to Fidel had appeared to be loyal to him before their defection. A policy that called for an outside invasion first and an internal rebellion afterward could never be sure of any rebellion.

Not only did the invasion come as a surprise but it discouraged the anti-Castro forces inside from doing anything until its nature and extent had become clear, and by then it was too late. No one would risk his life for an invasion that could not succeed because it was too small, or for an invasion that could succeed by itself because it had the full backing of the United States—and the latter was the first impression. Thus the invasion plan made the first stage of the battle a purely military one on a very limited terrain—a beachhead. It enabled Castro to concentrate overwhelming forces at a single point for a knockout blow.

The other course would have been to put the rebellion first and to hold an invasion in reserve to support an already existing popular movement, as Miró Cardona had explained in January, 1961, and as the "Confidential Bases" had implied in March. But the leaders of the Revolutionary Council were not strong or self-confident enough to insist in practice on what they had agreed on in principle. Some went along with the invasion because they had for many months given it their blessings, and others because they did not wish to open themselves to the charge that they had stood in the way of a possible victory. The two operations—the political, exemplified by the Revolutionary Council, and the military, represented by the invasion force—were kept so far apart that at least one portion of the Council knew little about the details of the invasion.

The situation in Cuba had been building up to some kind of popular explosion, but it could not be synchronized with the "deadline fixation," both Cuban and American. There was, of course, no guarantee that there would ever be a large-scale popular rebellion against Castro; the existing policy, however, had for many months not even encouraged one, politically or practically; and there were no guarantees about anything else. As long as the United States did not wish to be dragged into full-scale intervention, the priority for the anti-Castro forces in Cuba was a matter of necessity, not of choice. The Eisenhower Administration had not given the underground priority, and the Kennedy Administration ruled out full-scale intervention.

Yet, short of the Castro regime's collapse at the first blow from the outside, the invasion required a spontaneous outburst of popular support or an ever-increasing measure of American support. An invasion force that succeeded in overthrowing Castro without a demonstrative show of popular support could have ruled Cuba only in a state of perpetual civil war or as a thinly disguised American occupation. At best, it would have postponed another outbreak of *Fidelismo* for a few months or years. At worst, it could have made Cuba into another Algeria.

The alternative policy was formulated in the "Confidential Bases" but never really put into practice.

The "liberation" of Cuba wholly from the outside appealed mainly to those who were farthest removed from the Cuban people and had least faith in them. Yet Cuban history for a hundred years had been the story of recurrent tyranny—and recurrent struggle against tyranny. This has not been a people which has ever been subjugated for long without finding within itself the resources of heroism and sacrifice to renew the struggle. The true liberation of Cuba could not be achieved behind the backs of, and without the active participation of, the Cuban people in Cuba, and their participation could not be artificially manufactured or arbitrarily delegated.

THE MORNING AFTER

Failure, as well as success, can bring out fundamental attitudes and values not altogether clear in the course of the struggle, and the failure of Cochinos Bay—the Cubans prefer to call it after the beach where the invaders landed, Playa Girón—has brought them out in many quarters more sharply than ever before.

President Kennedy's first reaction expressed a determination not to accept the defeat as final and an intention to rethink the whole problem posed by Cuba. Perhaps the most significant feature of his speech on April 20, 1961, was the suggestion that the parts played by arms and politics in such a crisis urgently needed re-examination. If he seriously follows up his remark that "too long we have fixed our eyes on traditional military needs," more may have been gained from the Cuban defeat than lost.

The Republicans were somewhat inhibited from making political capital of the Cuban setback—despite the President's willingness to assume full responsibility for it—because of its peculiarly bipartisan ancestry. If the Cuban venture had proved a success, the Republicans might not have been able to resist pointing out that the Democrats had merely carried out what they had prepared for them, as Nixon did not fail to point out in the case of the first American astronaut.

Eisenhower's sense of fair play and national interest made him a model of discretion in this difficult moment, but Nixon could not altogether resist temptation. The former Vice President hinted broadly that "more power" should have been committed in Cuba to compensate for the mistaken intelligence estimates. This divergence may reflect more of a difference between Eisenhower and Nixon than between Kennedy and Eisenhower. It has been credibly reported that Nixon had once argued in favor of landing American forces in Cuba if the exiles could not make it on their own, and that Eisenhower had vetoed the proposal.

Among the Cuban exiles, the defeat had the effect of intensifying all the divisions that existed before. The Right and Center were overcome by pessimism bordering on despair, and publicly or privately expressed their belief in direct U.S. intervention as the only salvation. On the other hand, the anti-Castro Left, which had never believed in the precedence given to an armed invasion under U.S. auspices, was confirmed in its view. Because of this postinvasion schism, the MRP left the Cuban Revolutionary Council.

The invasion also provided Fidel Castro with the occasion for officially confirming the "socialist" character of the Cuban revolution. He actually did so for the first time on April 16, 1961, the day before the invasion, in a rather casual, mocking reference to the "imperialists": "That is what they cannot forgive—that we should be here under their nose and that we have effected a socialist revolution under the very nose of the United States."

In his speech on May 1, however, he made the pronouncement somewhat more formally: "Our deeds have signaled to the world the birth of a patriotic democratic and socialist revolution." What he meant by "socialist" he made sufficiently clear by hailing support from "the powerful socialist world, headed by the great Soviet Union and the People's Republic of China." After May 1, the term "socialist revolution" in Cuba became *de rigueur* to describe the Cuban revolution.

Che Guevara invented the theory, since repeated by innumerable epigoni, that the United States was responsible for Castro's actions or "responses," and presumably the latest coincidence between the frustrated invasion and Cuban "socialism" fits this pattern perfectly. In his book, *La Révolution Cubaine*, the French journalist Claude Julien expounds the view that the United States forced Castro to betray his own revolution to the Communists and Soviet Russia.

It is not necessary to exculpate the United States of

all blame or even a large share of the blame for the recent history of Cuba in order to feel, as I do, that this thesis is mistaken, profoundly mistaken. Fidel Castro and his inner circle have never been innocent victims of circumstances; they have always been the engine of this revolution in perpetual motion; they have leaped at one pretext or another to do what they wanted to do; they have incessantly increased their power by taking the initiative against their enemies and relentlessly pressing the advantage. A revolutionary leader does not betray the fundamental character of his revolution because American oil companies refuse to refine Soviet oil or because the United States suspends a sugar quota that has been attacked as "a symbol of colonialism." If he is really committed to a new social order different from capitalism and Communism, he does not resist the one by capitulating to the other with the speed of a push-button operation.

By waiting for the opportune occasion, every aggressive action can be made to appear in a defensive light, but history teaches us to look into the more obscure past for the deeper causes and motivations of such immediate and far-reaching "responses." In this case, as I have suggested, the decisive moves were made behind the scenes in 1959, and only their consequences were put on public display in 1960 and 1961.

No, Castro and his group have not merely been reacting to American moves, as if they were American puppets *manqués*, as if the United States always pulled the strings that forced them to do what they did not want to do or go where they did not want to go. This interpretation of the Castro revolution does not even do justice to its leader; it deprives him of any real control over his own revolution. There may be more than one way to explain why Castro betrayed the democratic revolution, and one of them is to blame the United States, but the betrayal is still no less a betrayal. I believe that the truth must be sought elsewhere, in the inner life and dynamism of *Fidelismo*.

THE DAY OF RECKONING

Only the ingenuous can still believe that Fidel Castro walked into a Communist trap or that he gave up the democratic road because the United States did not give him enough support in his early months in power. The Communists and Fidel walked toward each other, each with his eyes open, each filling a need in the other. The "trap theory" attributes a gullibility to Fidel which is again hardly fair to him. Official American offers might have embarrassed him a little more than the policy which respected his clearly understood preference for private rather than government forms of aid, but I fear that they would have accomplished little else. The $16-million credit the oil companies extended to Castro's Cuba did not save them from expropriation, and five or ten times that amount would not have bought them an indulgence. External circumstances influenced the Castro regime's methods and timing, but they did not determine its nature and direction.

The ordinary Western mind can only with the greatest difficulty comprehend the dynamism of this revolution. It was not made by a revolutionary party which had struggled for years to formulate an ideology and create an organization. It derives from twelve men who made their way to the Sierra Maestra mountains in December, 1956—less than six years ago!—and increased in number to only 180 in April, 1958—only four years ago! Their victory over Batista's bloated army and police was somewhat incredible, almost miraculous, and for them the miracles have not ceased.

It does not seem more farfetched that Cuba should set off a Latin American revolution than that the tiny group in the Sierra Maestra should have set off a Cuban revolution. To this must be added the conviction that the Cuban revolution cannot be finally victorious without a Latin American revolution, and that a Latin American revolution cannot be finally victorious without a revolution in the United States—an eventuality to which Fidel has made increasingly frequent allusions, only half in jest.

All this may be due to dizziness from success or illusions of grandeur, but the spirit of *Fidelismo* cannot be fathomed without taking it into account. The ideological and organizational vacuum of *Fidelismo* has been filled by Communism, which, in turn, has been given a new confidence and impetus by *Fidelismo*. As a result of this interpenetration, Cuba has begun to resemble every other Communist state in its essential political, economic, and ideological conformation; the "humanistic" improvisations of Castro's first year in power may soon seem just as far away as the Soviet's New Economic Policy of the 1920's seemed from Stalin's forced collectivization in the 1930's.

Whether the United States was wise to have suspended the sugar quota when it did is less important, in the long run, than that the suspension was the answer to a *Fidelista* prayer. The technique used to bring about the break of diplomatic relations—a forty-eight-hour demand for a drastic reduction of U.S. Embassy personnel—was similar. The dictate faced the United States with the choice of bowing to an ultimatum or going a step further and getting the inevitable over with quickly. Short of utter capitulation, I cannot conceive of any U.S. policy that would have satisfied the souls of Fidel, Raúl, and "El Che."

For those who desire, condone, or ignore the Communist conquest of Cuba, the April, 1961, invasion presented no difficult problem. They could gloat over the failure or enjoy an orgy of *Schadenfreude*. Some could do so, however, only by deceiving themselves about the reality of Communist influence in Cuba. But the day of reckoning had to come. At the present rate of *Fidelista*-Communist fusion (May, 1961), they will soon have to recognize that reality or risk making laughingstocks of themselves. And if they do not go along to the bitter end, they too will know what it means to be "betrayed" by Fidel Castro; he may even ridicule them on television if they should make nuisances of themselves complaining of their disillusionment.

"Nonintervention" also presented them with no great problem. As long as the only intervention was by definition United States, everything became absurdly simple. But the Cuban revolution has never been that simple. It has never been contained within the borders of Cuba. In 1955, Castro used Mexico as the training ground for his invasion force. He set up an organization in the United States to collect funds and recruit volunteers. In March, 1958, President José Figueres of Costa Rica permitted arms to be sent to Castro's forces in the Sierra Maestra. To overthrow Batista, Castro accepted aid wherever he could get it. If the same stringent rules were applied to him as some have tried to apply to his present enemies, Batista might still be in power.

Since 1959, Castro has been intervening flagrantly throughout Latin America. In November, 1960, young anti-Castro Cubans broke into the Cuban Embassy in Lima, Peru, and forced the Chargé d'Affaires to give them a file of documents marked "Strictly Confidential." Photostats of these documents have been published, and the then Secretary of the Embassy, Andrés Quintín Noas, now in exile, has confirmed their authenticity. One letter, dated October 4, 1960, from Ambassador Luis Ricardo Alonso to Raúl Castro, reported the payment of $15,000 (427,500 Peruvian soles) to eight professors, sixteen newspapers and magazines, fifteen labor unions, and ten political organizations, and another $15,000 to the Communist Party in thirteen Peruvian cities and towns. All the names and amounts were carefully recorded. As a result of this evidence, Peru broke diplomatic relations with Cuba.

Intervention can take many forms—from the Castro regime's vicious war of nerves against the admirable administration of Governor Luis Muñoz Marín in Puerto

Rico to the Soviet bloc's huge investment of arms and manipulation of a servile Cuban Communist Party. Much of what passes for "nonintervention" in the Cuban civil war is, in practice, an acceptance of unilateral Soviet intervention.

For those who do not desire to or cannot ignore the Communist conquest of Cuba, the present situation poses difficult and complex problems. The invasion was indefensible in conception as well as execution, but much of the criticism has been transmuted into support or apologetics for Castro's regime. In the end, the most unfortunate result of the fiasco may be that the guilt arising out of it has sought an outlet in tolerance for and subtle identification with an onrushing totalitarianism. I have never heard an argument in favor of the Cuban dictatorship—from the uselessness of elections to the mistreatment of the Cuban peasants who constituted about one-third of the nation—which could not be applied with slight modifications to virtually every other country. Some of the criticisms of the invasion require at least as much criticism as the invasion itself.*

I cannot separate the politics of arms from the arms

* This is particularly true of the "Open Letter to President Kennedy" drafted by a few members of the Harvard faculty and signed by seventy intellectuals in the Boston area, as published in *The New York Times*, May 10, 1961. If it were merely an anti-invasion appeal, I would have no quarrel with it. But it goes much further afield and betrays such curious squeamishness in its references to the character of the Castro regime, such superficiality in its explanation of the "sharp increase in the power of the local Communist Party," and such gullibility in its recommendations for detaching the Castro regime from the Communist bloc, that one wonders whether many of its distinguished signatories have devoted much time or energy to a study of recent Cuban history. It is not a little disquieting that almost none of these seventy signatories has been moved to express publicly his subsequent attitude toward the development of Castro's regime.

of politics. The politics of the arms that went into the invasion of Cochinos Bay made the failure a costly defeat and would have made the success a Pyrrhic victory. But to say this and no more is to doom in advance the prospect of any future anti-Castro opposition, even the most democratic. These arms were used badly, but any politics in Cuba today demands arms. Castro cannot be overthrown except by force, just as there was no other way to overthrow Batista. When Castro sentenced Matos to twenty years' imprisonment, he served notice on all opposition to go underground and fight force with force or submit without a struggle. As long as there are men and women in Cuba who believe in civil liberties, representative government, land reform instead of Soviet-style state farms, freedom of expression, association with the democratic West, and free trade unions, there will be an underground, and despite the present setback, it will revive and grow. If no one else will provide the necessary conditions for its growth, Castro and the Communists will do so.

But no anti-Castro movement can resist Russian tanks and Czechoslovak machine guns with sympathy alone. It would be more humane and more honest to advise any movement not to resist than to resist with bare hands. Castro's democratic opponents have the right and the duty to obtain arms where they can, as Castro did and as other revolutionary movements have done. The United States can help, but a democratic Cuban opposition worthy of the name will accept arms or other assistance only on its own terms. Whatever the United States or any other power does or does not do must influence the situation in Cuba; the United States could remove its influence only by disappearing. Some forms of "nonintervention" are nothing more than acquiescence in someone else's intervention, and some forms of "intervention" are so wrong and futile that they amount in their practical effect to nonintervention.

In and through Cuba, I fear, we are reliving many of the problems that plagued us in the era of Hitler and Stalin. Hitler never permitted us to forget the crimes of the Versailles Treaty, the weaknesses of the Weimar Republic, and the millions of unemployed. The Bolsheviks never permitted us to forget the dark Czarist past. The *Líder Máximo* never permits us to forget the evils of imperialism, the misdeeds of previous democratic governments, and the poverty of the Cuban peasants. But the avenger of Versailles, the gravedigger of Weimar, and the savior of the unemployed was also a demonic nihilist who inflicted such degradation on his own people and infamies on other peoples that they cannot even now be uttered without sickening us. The absolute power of one party degenerated into the absolute power of one man, and that man degenerated into a psychopathic executioner of millions, among them his own comrades. The totalitarian disease in Germany and Russia did not strike in all its virulence at once; it crept up on its victims in stages; it came sugar-coated as national liberation and economic development. In the end, however, one thing mattered more than all else—the capacity for evil of these all-embracing, insatiable, suffocating tyrannies grew with their accretion of power. Each generation, it seems, must learn the lesson in its own way. Unfortunately, this lesson is always an expensive one.

III. CASTRO AND COMMUNISM

As Fidel Castro has often said, and his admirers have endlessly repeated, the Cuban revolution is a "process." The process has been made up of "stages," which have succeeded one another with dizzying rapidity. Each stage has told us more and more, but no stage has told us so much about the whole process as has the latest one.

The previous stage, which began about the time of the doomed invasion, was complicated by a peculiarly Cuban problem: How could there be a "socialist revolution" without a ruling "socialist party"? The announcement of Cuba's "socialist revolution" was made by Castro on April 16, the day before the invasion, in an offhand, almost accidental way. He repeated it more fully and formally on May 1, but the former date has gained recognition as the official inauguration of the new era. For the more orthodox Cuban Communists, however, the real transition to the "socialist revolution" had come six months earlier, on October 13, 1960, when 382 business enterprises, almost all of them Cuban, were nationalized.

In any case, the announcement of the "socialist revolution" in April, 1961, gave a new and sharper urgency to the problem that had been creeping up since the previous August. At that time, General Secretary Blas Roca of the official Communist PSP had presented in his main report to its Eighth Congress the perspective of a "complete union" or "fusion" of all the revolutionary forces "in a single movement." For about fourteen months, this proposal was undoubtedly the most delicate subject in Cuban politics. No other matter was treated with more caution in Cuba or generated more rumors outside Cuba.

The question of "the party" had long puzzled observers of this seemingly nonconformist revolution. Before taking power, Castro had again and again promised full restoration of the rights of political parties, as provided in the 1940 Constitution. For example, in one of the key documents of this period, his letter of December 14, 1957, to the Cuban exiles, he had pledged himself to uphold the "right" of political parties, even during the provisional government, to present their programs before the people, organize the citizenry, and participate in general elections. But after he took power, nothing of the sort happened. With the exception of the PSP, none of the former parties reorganized, and no new parties emerged, not even Castro's own 26th of July Movement. He stubbornly insisted on keeping the latter an amorphous, largely personal instrument. He refused to intervene when his own 26th of July associates came to him to protest against the substitution of PSP members for 26th of July men in positions of authority. And those who protested soon found themselves out of favor with Castro himself. On these occasions, which were not infrequent in the first months, Fidel would feign surprise, blame Raúl Castro or Che Guevara, break out into a tirade against the Communists, exclaim that they were getting under his skin and that he did not intend to put up with their encroachments much longer. These private assurances on his part kept many worried 26th of July leaders in line, and they in turn would communicate their confidence in Fidel's ultimate loyalties. By the end of 1959, however, it was clear that Fidel's first loyalties were to Raúl and Che and, with them or through them, to the Communists.

When Jean-Paul Sartre and Simone de Beauvoir visited Cuba, early in 1960, they were struck by the absence of, as they put it, "cadres" and an "apparatus." They were told that the 26th of July Movement had had an apparatus but that it had been permitted to lapse because it had been too "petty bourgeois" and could not keep pace with the radicalization of the revolution. This explanation seems to have satisfied them, but it did not satisfy me when I visited Cuba soon after, because everyone I met in any position of authority was obviously petty bourgeois in origin, and no class distinction could be made between those who had lost their positions and those who had replaced them. Nevertheless, M. Sartre and Mme. de Beauvoir came to Cuba looking for an ideology and a party, and when they found neither, or at least neither in a recognizable form, they were intrigued and delighted. The absence of an official ideology and a party became an earnest of the Cuban revolution's originality, and without this appearance of novelty and nonconformity, it is doubtful that so many observers would have lost their heads over it. Some of the most eloquent pages in C. Wright Mills's *Listen, Yankee!* commanded sympathy and respect precisely because his Cubans seemed so fresh, so *sui generis* in the way they told off both capitalists and Communists, so innocent that they did not know what to call themselves. Mills himself put his own judgment to the test by assuring his readers that "the leading men of Cuba's Government are not 'Communist,' or even Communist-type," as he had experienced Communism in Latin America or the Soviet Union. I am not sure I know what a "Communist-type" is, but I do know that the most unlikely types have become Communists as long as they wanted to do so badly enough; and of those cited by Professor Mills as his sources, with but one exception all of them have done their best to demonstrate that they are, if not Communists, at least "Communist-types."

The exception is the former Minister of Communications, Enrique Oltuski, whom Sartre called "one of our best friends" and to whom he devoted an entire article. Oltuski, indeed, played an outstanding role in gaining the sympathy of foreign observers for the Cuban revolution. In my case, I went to his office one morning expecting to talk to him for a half-hour or so, but he kept me until seven that evening, talking, talking, talking. When I complained at about three in the afternoon that I needed some lunch, he told me that he had lost the habit of eating lunch during his underground days against Batista, and I survived the day only because he offered me the ice cream and milk which his secretary eventually brought for him. Oltuski was the very archetype of a young and ardent *Fidelista,* only twenty-nine then, the son of Polish-Jewish immigrant parents who had managed to send him through an engineering school in Florida. He must have talked to me the way he talked to Sartre and Mills, because I heard his voice through many of their pages, earnestly scorning the Cuban Communists, discussing the relative merits of capitalist America and Communist Russia, and rejecting both in favor of building, in Professor Mills's words, "a brand-new social and economic order in Cuba."

Oltuski was removed as Minister of Communications in the early summer of 1960 and given a lesser post in the agrarian-reform organization, INRA, which itself was being sharply downgraded in importance. He then shifted over from the industrial department of INRA to Guevara's Ministry of Industries, and Guevara seems to have taken on the task of domesticating and rehabilitating this type of wavering and "immature" *Fidelista.* The former Minister, Faustino Pérez, who resigned in 1959, has also apparently worked his way back into the good graces of the present ruling group. Oltuski's story, however, is not an individual one and therein lies its significance. He belonged to a group of *Fidelistas* who believed devoutly in Fidel and in the search for a new path toward "liberty with bread and without terror." When Fidel once said that "capitalism may kill man with hunger" and "Communism kills man by wiping out his freedom," they believed him. For them this meant that the *Fidelistas* could "use" the Communists but could never embrace Communism or merge with the Communists. By the summer of 1960, however, they were faced with a shattering crisis of conscience. They could no longer deny to themselves that Fidel was heading toward a fusion with the Communists, and yet they could not bring themselves to oppose him. In similar circumstances, others turned against Fidel. But this group was immobilized by what it considered to be the fatal choice between Castro's emergent Communism and American imperialism. Since this stage of the process was well advanced by August, 1960, the month Professor Mills spent in Cuba and, incidentally, the same month that Blas Roca had set in motion the "united party," it was cruelly ironic to read so many of the anachronistic sentiments of the Oltuskis in *Listen, Yankee!* after they had stopped speaking that way.

THE NEW PARTY

Nevertheless, the "united party" was not an easy problem. Ostensibly, it was supposed to merge the 26th of July Movement, the student Directorio Revolucionario, and the Communist PSP. But the 26th of July had long been gutted, and the Directorio enjoyed an even more shadowy existence. They were no match for the PSP, which, as Blas Roca boasted at the Eighth Congress, could have multiplied its members "several times." The proposal of fusion, then, concerned primarily the PSP and the top leadership, which had hitherto been identified, for want of any better name, as *Fidelistas.* In effect, the crucial questions were: How would Fidel fit into a single, ruling state party, and would Cuba be transformed into a party state?

In essence, it was necessary to fit Fidel and his personal group into a Communist Party without saddling them with the dubious record of the existing Communist Party, the PSP, which could never live down its years of intimate alliance and partnership with the former dictator, Fulgencio Batista. According to the Communist line, there had been two Batistas, the "good" Batista with whom they were intimately allied from the end of 1938 to the beginning of 1946 and the "bad" Batista who had seized power in 1952. Castro, like his former political mentor, Eduardo Chibás, had never recognized this distinction and had reviled Batista, without too much historical verisimilitude, as always a bloody and hated tyrant. The PSP had never been able to cleanse itself of its pro-Batista past, and from the first, Castro's extreme toleration, if not active encouragement, of Batista's former partners was not easy for him to explain away.

Yet the solution was indicated in the PSP's own past. Its first incarnation was as the Communist Party of Cuba, founded in 1925. Blas Roca had joined the party in 1929 and had become General Secretary in 1934. All the other top leaders also went back to the 1920's or 1930's, which made them total products of the Stalinist school of Communist leadership. For about a quarter of a century, in good times and bad, through all the twists and turns, they had stuck it out together, with Blas Roca a kind of Cuban Thorez, never admired for his personal brilliance but indispensable for his Muscovite loyalty and dependable opportunism. The Communist Party of Cuba changed its name to Unión Revolucionaria Comunista in 1940 in an effort, not unlike the present one, to enlarge itself, and to the Partido Socialista Popular in 1944 in another tactical maneuver. Thus there was no lack of precedent in the party's own history to rebaptize itself in order to make a fresh start.

Fidel could not simply join the PSP without losing face. Blas Roca admitted at the Eighth Congress that Fidel had been right about waging an armed struggle against Batista, though he somewhat spoiled the effect by taking Fidel to task in the same sentence for not having given enough attention "to other aspects of the struggle." But Blas Roca had also stoutly defended the Communists' seven-year alliance with Batista previously, as Fidel could not do without risking stultification. Nor was there any fitting place for a *Líder Máximo* in the PSP's long-established hierarchy. A new organization, which did not have to carry the burden of the PSP's long and checkered history, was obviously preferable. For the old-time Communists, it would be their fourth incarnation, and for the *Fidelistas,* their integration into the Communist movement with the least possible damage to their *amour-propre.* Above all, it could be presented to the masses as Fidel Castro's party and not as the party that Fidel took over from Blas Roca.

The way the new party was introduced to the public shows how these matters are handled in Cuba. There was no open discussion of the nature or leadership of the new party. The news was broken piecemeal, always as accomplished facts or pronouncements from on high. On May 24, 1961, the semiofficial organ *Revolución* published on a back page two photographs of a meeting in the town of Guantánamo with a few lines identifying them as the scene of the fusion between the PSP, 26th of July, and Directorio Revolucionario. Thus one could gather that fusion was taking place on a local scale. On June 4, at a student meeting in Havana, Guevara was asked about the progress of the revolutionary process despite the absence of a mass party. The party existed in the real unity of the revolutionary organizations, he explained, though it had not yet been organized. And he added that "the only thing lacking is to create the party and to name Fidel as its Secretary General." This for the first time intimated that Fidel's role in the new party had already been decided or at least that a position on it had been taken by those close to him. Not until June was it made known that the new party would be organized in two phases, a preparatory one to be known as the Organizaciones Revolucionarias Integradas (Integrated Revolutionary Organizations), or ORI, and a final one to be called the Partido Unido de la Revolución Socialista (United Party of the Socialist Revolution), or PURS. The leadership of the ORI was never formally disclosed; it trickled out bit by bit as leaders of the PSP, including Blas Roca, suddenly appeared in print as "leaders of the ORI."

The same procedure was followed with the program of the new party. Late in August, an ORI spokesman, Captain Emilio Aragonés, announced: "The United Party of the Revolution will be built on Marxist-Leninist principles." On the organizational side, he stated, the party would be based on "democratic centralism," which he explained as follows:

> Democratic centralism is the method which Lenin discovered for the application of true democracy. It is the only method for applying democracy. It consists of democracy being applied by a central leadership. An idea approved by the masses is applied by a centralized leadership, by the leadership of the workers' vanguard which is the Party [*Revolución*, August 21, 1961].

After this, all the "mass organizations," such as the Asociación de Jóvenes Rebeldes, followed suit, and its leader solemnly declared that "our organization is converting itself into one of the Marxist-Leninist pillars of our revolution" (*Revolución*, September 23, 1961).

And this is how official Marxism-Leninism came to Cuba.

New party or old, however, there still remained the subtle transmutation of Fidel Castro into a Communist. After all, he had protested for years that he was no Communist; he had, from time to time and as late as 1959, said some harsh things about Communism; his propagandists and sympathizers had long risen in all their righteous wrath at the slightest imputation that he was, might be, or could become a Communist. Obviously, some explanation was necessary. Had he always been, as many of his enemies had charged, a secret Communist? Or was he a more or less recent convert? He was, in effect, faced with the choice of having been a political fraud or, as he himself came close to saying, a political fool.

So troublesome and ticklish was this transfiguration that it took an entire year to manage. I became conscious of it for the first time in the interview the Italian Communist organ *L'Unità* published on February 1, 1961. In it, Castro struck an unfamiliar pose of humility before the official Cuban Communists, whom he defended for having previously distrusted his guerrilla fighters, who, he said penitentially, had been "full of petty-bourgeois prejudices and defects." Again, at a banquet in honor of the Communist organ *Hoy*, on March 25, 1961, he was curiously apologetic about the weakness of the revolution's leaders "in the ideological sphere." As the months passed, he seemed to become afflicted with a rash of modesty, never before one of his outstanding characteristics. He confided to a television audience that, at the time of Batista's fall, "we did not know much but we were full of good will" (*Revolución*, April 10, 1961). In a revealing speech to intellectuals, he explained or complained that the Cuban revolution did not have the "gestation period which other revolutions have had" and that the Cuban leaders did not have the "intellectual maturity which the leaders of other revolutions have had." Despite their important contribution, he went on, "we do not consider ourselves theorists of revolutions nor intellectuals of revolutions" (*Revolución*, June 30, 1961). An American admirer quoted him as saying in this period: "We had so many silly ideas. I had so many silly ideas, my head, there was so much crap in it."*

For several months, then, the answer Castro seemed to give to the question about his conversion to Communism

* Carl Marzani, *Mainstream*, May, 1961, p. 29.

was that it had been more or less recent. He never claimed that he had been a Communist incognito or that he had been a Communist in all but name. He paid homage to the Communists, as if to explain why he had decided to become one. His speeches changed character and parts of them began to read like the ABC of "Marxism-Leninism." When he exhorted, "It is necessary to study and to learn constantly in order to be able to find the correct explanation, the clear explanation, the Marxist-Leninist explanation of the problems" (*Revolución*, November 11, 1961), one felt that Fidel himself had been studying and learning.

FROM DEPENDENCE TO DEPENDENCE

Meanwhile, other forces were pressing in the direction of the new party. The most important was the changeover from a *Fidelista* economy to a Communist economy.

In the first year or year and a half of the revolution, economic policy was primarily dominated by political considerations. It had many attractive features, though it was apt to make professional economists wonder how long it could last. When Castro said that the Cuban revolution was different in that it did not intend to sacrifice the present generation for future generations, as he implied the Russian revolution had done, he seemed as good as his word. Large sums were spent on housing, beaches, schools, and various types of public works mainly designed to soak up the unemployed. These investments paid off prodigiously in popular support, but they were largely "nonproductive" in economic terms. The reduction of rents and increases of salary in 1959 stimulated consumption, but they were clearly short-term measures and had begun to exhaust themselves by the spring of 1960. By this time, however, Castro's regime was ready for the next stage, which took the form of a break with the United States that summer and nationalization in the fall.

When the United States embargoed almost all trade with Cuba in October, 1960, the Cuban attitude was one of "good riddance." Guevara, then head of the National Bank, declared that Cuba would not be seriously harmed by the embargo because she was prepared for it and because black-marketeers in the United States would defy it. He did not deny that there might be economic difficulties, but he asked the people to show their "confidence in the solidarity of the nations that have offered to stand by us." These nations of the Soviet bloc, with whom Guevara soon made one trade agreement after another, rapidly replaced the United States as Cuba's chief source of exports and imports. The removal of Cuba from the American economic sphere of influence did not mean the economic liberation of Cuba; it merely exchanged dependence on the United States for dependence on the Soviet bloc. Cuban imports from the Soviet bloc shot up from only 2 million pesos in 1959, to 136 million in 1960, to an estimated 580 million in 1961. In 1958, the last year before Castro, Cuban imports from the United States had amounted to 542 million pesos, or 69.8 per cent of the total. In the middle of 1960, after the reduction of the sugar quota,

75.1 per cent of Cuba's exports went to non-Communist countries and 24.9 per cent to Communist countries; in 1961, the official estimates are 74.6 per cent to Communist countries and 25.4 per cent to non-Communist countries. Cuba has undoubtedly become more dependent on the Soviet bloc than it was formerly on the United States.

This dependence on countries thousands of miles away has, in a sense, created an economic monstrosity. As Guevara admitted early in January, 1961, the Soviets produce more sugar than Cuba and, therefore, do not need what Cuba has chiefly to offer. They were willing to give the Cubans advantageous terms, he said, only for "political" reasons. The Chinese, he said, went the Russians one better and told him that Cuba should pay for her imports whenever she could, or if she could not pay, that would be of "no importance." The change-over from American to Soviet-bloc machines and parts has, of course, caused enormous dislocations. The breakdown of American equipment became so acute that a campaign was started for workers to "construct your own machine." Guevara told a conference on production in August, 1961, that the reserves of raw materials were so low that the slightest trouble on the high seas brought on some kind of crisis, and "any delay of a couple of boats provokes the paralyzation of many industries." He added: "Furthermore, we are in a perennial crisis in spare parts."

On the other hand, a faithful reader of the Cuban press might well live in a state of permanent euphoria. A day seems wasted without quotas overfulfilled, progress reports on all fronts, figures that boast of more and more and better and better. If one could eat figures, the Cuban people would easily be the best fed in the world. But on closer examination, the figures usually refer to something that is going to happen in the future. Guevara and others, who should know, also have a disconcerting habit of complaining about "the lack of data" and "extreme laxness" in statistics.* If everything is getting better and better, it is hard to account for the drastic change of line in the Castro regime's appeal to the masses. By 1961, Castro and other leaders had begun to urge them to live for the future, not the present. "We have to live in love with the future," Fidel said in May. "Do not think so much in the present as in the future" (*Revolución,* May 15, 1961). His brother, Raúl, reiterated: "It should not be thought that our struggle is for today, nor is it for tomorrow; our struggle is for the future, for our children" (*Revolución,* July 27, 1961). By the time the August, 1961, production conference was held, Fidel had to call on the people "to sacrifice" (*Obra Revolucionaria,* August 26, 1961), and in October, he referred to the present generation as "generous, stoical, sacrificing" (*Revolución,* October 25, 1961).

The full import of nationalization also took some time to sink in. About 80 per cent of Cuban industry had been nationalized in a short time, and the figure has now

* *Obra Revolucionaria,* August 26, 1961, and *Revolución,* September 25, 1961. The discrepancies between various types of figures, and between some figures and statements by government leaders, are shrewdly analyzed by Boris Goldenberg in "La revolución agraria cubana," *Cuadernos,* February, 1962, pp. 54–56.

risen to 90 per cent. Administratively and technically, Cuba was almost totally unprepared for the new order. The old state bureaucracy had been dismantled *in toto* and a new one hastily improvised. By the end of 1960, a large part of Cuba's administrative and technical personnel had fled into exile. The desperate effort made by Castro's regime to train a new generation of Cuban administrators and technicians could barely begin to fill the need. Soviet-bloc technicians and "advisers" flocked in, and experts were recruited from all over Latin America, the latter attracted by higher salaries than they could command at home. Nevertheless, the shortage of skilled administrative and technical personnel has been one of the foremost sources of frustration and failure. In effect, Castro's Cuba has at its disposal far fewer administrators and technicians than pre-Castro Cuba had, and has undertaken to build a collective economy, which would require far more.

HAVANA'S MEDICINE

That the Castro regime was heading into trouble was apparent by the end of 1960. A decline from their previous standard of living was felt first, apart from the former property owners, by the professionals and industrial workers. As early as April to June of 1960, a veteran anarchosyndicalist, Agustín Souchy, no friend of the United States or capitalism, visited Cuba and estimated that about 60–70 per cent of the people supported Castro. "In many nationalized enterprises," he reported, "salaries were cut, and various social improvements, obtained by years of struggle, reduced."* In December, 1960, Castro and other Cuban leaders made speeches to groups of professionals and workers that clearly indicated how worried they were. But the invasion fiasco in April, 1961, reversed the trend and again consolidated the regime's popular support. Indeed, the victory was so complete and the opposition so stunned that anything seemed possible, and the whole economic and political program was accelerated.

Nevertheless, serious shortages began to appear in the early summer of 1961. Fats and meat became particularly scarce and often unobtainable, especially in the cities. Yet Cuba's per capita consumption of edible lard and fats had been one of the highest in the world, and she had been an *exporter* of meat.† Other shortages became so severe that housewives were forced to spend hours in queues, frequently leaving empty-handed because the supplies had run out before they were reached. The situation became so critical that it could no longer be ignored in the press, and *Revolución* of July 13, 1961, carried a front-page story that the price of pork had risen "astronomically" but that the authorities had stepped in to regulate it. Since then, essential foods and goods seem to become available intermittently, provoke runs on the stores, and disappear as suddenly as they appcar. At the same time, workers' absenteeism began, as Guevara put it, to take on "alarming characteristics,"

* *Testimonios sobre la Revolución Cubana* (Buenos Aires: Editorial Reconstruir, 1960), pp. 62 and 65.

† The per capita consumption of edible lard and fats in Cuba was equal to that of the U.S. and Belgium and greater than that of Switzerland or France! (*Revolución*, May 15, 1961).

and he attacked it as "the darkest, most subtle form of counterrevolutionary activity" (*Revolución*, September 25, 1961). Minister of Foreign Affairs Raúl Roa declared that "absenteeism is not only vagrancy or negligence; it is linked with the *gusanería* and the counterrevolution" (*Verde Olivo*, November 5, 1961).* Doctors were threatened with severe sentences if they falsely helped workers to give illness as an excuse for absences, a common practice in the past.

Castro and other spokesmen have offered various explanations for these shortages and difficulties. Production has increased, but it has not been able to keep pace with demand. The once derided American embargo has become an "imperialist blockade," responsible for most of Cuba's ills. The long boat hauls from the Soviet Union and China, the necessity to adapt Cuban production to the technology of the Soviet bloc and to tie the entire Cuban economy into the bloc's planning systems, the shortage of administrative and technical personnel, inexperience, and errors have also been blamed. Whatever the full truth may be, the revolution has undoubtedly done least for and taken most from the middle class and industrial workers in the urban centers, especially the capital.

Castro himself referred somewhat scornfully to the state of mind in the capital: "Above all, in Havana, a phenomenon became noticeable—a great vacillation of

* The favorite term of abuse in Castro's Cuba is "*gusano*" ("worm"). It has even been made into a generic form, "*gusanería*," and applied to anyone or anything the regime considers an enemy. Thus, Guevara could think of nothing more offensive to say of the late Dag Hammarskjöld than to call him, after his death, "*un servil gusano imperialista*"—"a servile, imperialist worm" (*Revolución*, October 30, 1961).

opinion. So much so that every two weeks it was necessary to talk to them as if one were giving them a dose of medicine" (*Revolución*, November 11, 1961). But he blamed the "phenomenon" on the "great mass of petty bourgeoisie" in Havana. Later that month, however, Guevara admitted that there had been many times when the working class "gave the impression that it did not understand the new role which it had to play." An "invisible barrier," as he put it, had existed between the revolutionary administration and the workers in general, which had been broken through only a very few months before. It was no secret, he said, that the oil, electrical, and telephone workers had not directly benefited economically from the revolution, which had occupied itself with the less privileged. He mentioned that there had been more grave work accidents in the mines during the revolutionary administration than during the previous private administration. And he revealed the "sad reality" that it would be "years" before the workers in the basic sugar industry could be paid more (*Revolución*, November 29, 1961).

Early in 1962, Guevara was the bearer of even more depressing news. He let it be known on January 27 that the basic sugar industry had been going from bad to worse. It appeared that the 1961 sugar crop had been very poorly harvested owing to too great dependence on voluntary labor, much of which did more harm than good. Guevara attributed the major difficulties to "disorganization" and drought, and he lamented the fact that the amount of cane cut per unit of land had taken such a sharp drop that the Cuban yield had fallen to among the lowest of the great sugar-producing countries (*Bohemia*, February 4, 1962). Guevara's report was only one of several indications of an increasing crisis in Castro's agrarian-reform program. This crisis has apparently been caused by general mismanagement, experimental fiascoes, premature allocations of forces and funds to industrialization rather than agriculture, and the devious resistance of the *campesinos* to state control.

The agricultural crisis was officially recognized in February, 1962, by the appointment of a top Communist leader, Carlos Rafael Rodríguez, as President of the many-tentacled INRA, a position formerly occupied by Fidel Castro himself. This shift was accompanied by admissions of a "supply crisis" and a severe "shortage of consumer goods," including such things as *plátanos* (a form of banana), *boniatos* (sweet potatoes), and *malangas* (a vegetable plant), which had always been plentiful in the diets of rural Cubans. The food shortage, in particular, had become so widespread and extreme that the former explanation that it had been due to increased consumption could no longer convince or deceive anyone. The crisis had basically originated in the spheres of production and distribution and, most acutely, in the sphere that was supposed to be most distinctive and triumphant in Castro's revolution—agrarian reform. On taking over the INRA post, Carlos Rafael said: "The sowing, the different breeds of cattle, and the whole agricultural economy are in a quite critical situation. We will attempt to correct the errors that have been committed until now."

In the earlier stages of the Cuban revolution, its

leaders would have tossed off these troubles with romantic bravado and gone on to muddle through. But something new has been added, and the old ways will no longer work. The new element is the Four-Year Plan, which was initiated in 1962, the "*Año de la Planificación.*" In classical socialism, certain social and economic prerequisites came before the plan. In Cuba, the plan must create the prerequisites. This type of inverted "socialism" has its own laws and logic, and even free and easy Cuba cannot be immune to them. There are "norms" and "goals" that each worker, each factory, each industry must meet. "Socialist competition" has come to Cuba, where it has been relabeled "*Emulación.*" The most important task of the trade unions, Guevara has made clear, is to stimulate "emulation" and increase production (*Revolución*, November 29, 1961). "Productivity" has become the battle cry and "improvisation" the enemy.

"Remember, we are not going through any Stalinist kind of forced industrialization," warned Professor Mills's Cuban in the summer of 1960. That was true in 1959 and most of 1960, less true in 1961, but it is totally untrue today. For whatever reason and whatever justification, Castro's Cuba has entered the stage of *forced industrialization.* Speech after speech and action after action have made this clear. It explains why there has been such emphasis on sacrificing for the future, working harder for the same or less pay, productivity at all cost, and fetishism of the plan. Since Cuba does not have a fraction of the raw materials and human resources that Soviet Russia had, the Cuban experience will probably be no easier or gentler. And these extreme economic changes could not be carried out without extreme political changes.

THE WORD GAME

For those who had been following Cuban events closely in 1961, the adoption of Marxism-Leninism as the official ideology, the nature of the new party, and the fusion of *Fidelismo* and Communism had been foreshadowed for months. One telltale sign, for example, was the editorial board of the new party's monthly organ, *Cuba Socialista*, the first issue of which appeared in September, 1961. The board is composed of Prime Minister Fidel Castro, President Osvaldo Dorticós, Blas Roca, Carlos Rafael Rodríguez, and Fabio Grobart, the East-European–born mystery man of Cuban Communism, who had been forced to leave Cuba some years ago and made his reappearance from East Europe last year. Since Dorticós was once a Communist and had come back into the fold, the ratio was three or four "old Communists" to one "new Communist"—a fair approximation of the distribution in the coming top leadership. The magazine is almost an exact replica in its contents of the former PSP monthly organ, *Fundamentos*, which it has replaced. The first number of *Cuba Socialista* contained contributions by Castro, Dorticós, and Blas Roca, but by the third number, only former PSP leaders, a Dominican Republic Communist, and two Soviet writers filled its pages. Since all the other members of the editorial board are so busy with other things, Grobart is the actual director and, again, the *éminence grise* of Cuban Communism.

The relations of the new party to the world Communist movement and to Soviet Russia were further clarified at the Twenty-second Congress of the Soviet Communist Party, in October, 1961. The Cuban delegation of five was headed by Blas Roca, and included the Minister of Labor, Augusto Martínez Sánchez; the Cuban Ambassador in Moscow, Faure Chomón; Captain Emilio Aragonés; and a woman, Rita Díaz. They officially represented the ORI, which confirmed the understanding that it was just another Communist Party (*Revolución*, October 16, 1961). In his speech to the Congress, Blas Roca lined up unconditionally with the Russians against the Albanians. He joined in the denunciation of "revisionism and dogmatism," the current Soviet ideological stigmata for the Yugoslavs and Chinese. According to the text in *Pravda* of October 23, he declared: "We, in full accord with our conviction and experience, firmly support the position set forth by Comrade Khrushchev with respect to the negative actions of the leaders of the Albanian Party of Labor." At the conclusion of Blas Roca's speech, Khrushchev cried out: "Hail the leader of the Cuban revolution, Fidel Castro! Hail the Cuban delegation headed by Comrade Blas Roca!" At the November 7 celebration of the anniversary of the Bolshevik revolution, Blas Roca was placed next to Ho Chi Minh, who stood next to Khrushchev on the reviewing stand.

Very little, too, had been left to the imagination regarding the ideology and organization of the new party.

After Captain Aragonés' statement in August, 1961, Antonio Núñez Jiménez, Executive Director of INRA, was quoted from Prague two months later to the effect that the PURS "will be a Marxist-Leninist party, based on the principles of democratic centralism" (*Revolución*, October 25, 1961). And various old-time PSP leaders have been busy delivering disquisitions on the exact meaning of "democratic centralism," the role of the "vanguard," and the selection of party members.

Another source of enlightenment was a recent speech by Castro to the First Congress of the Responsables del Trabajo de Orientación Revolucionaria—those responsible for the work of "revolutionary orientation." Most interesting was not his disclosure that he had become a student and devotee of Marxism-Leninism—he had left no doubt about that before—but rather his explanation of why Cuba would have "orientators" and "revolutionary instructors" instead of "commissars," "agitators," and "propagandists." The passage is so suggestive of what promises to be the original element in Castro's Communism that it is worth savoring in full:

> The commissar is not a commissar, he is a "revolutionary instructor"—although, sincerely, the word "commissar" is a very nice word. The former agitator and propagandist are no longer an agitator and a propagandist; we would do wrong if we should say "the agitator," and call you "agitators" or "propagandists," because it seems to us that this word belongs more to the period of struggle for the conquest of power, when it was necessary to agitate.
>
> There are other times when it is necessary to awaken the revolutionary spirit. Then it is right. And above

all, it is necessary to orientate. The word "to indoctrinate" is not good. What impression does it give? It makes one feel that you are inculcating something in the head of an individual by dint of repeating things, that he is an individual who has nothing in his head and that you are stuffing it into him, as if the strings of a puppet were being manipulated, and ideas were being stuffed into his head. Then he would say: "They won't indoctrinate me."

The "revolutionary instructor" is a word which is the substitute for "indoctrinator"; "the orientator" is the substitute for "the agitator," and does the same thing. Just imagine if we would call the national organization the "National Commission of Revolutionary Agitation" [laughter]. Therefore, words are being substituted. These are words which have infuriated the enemy [*Revolución*, November 11, 1961].

This game of "word substitution" bids fair to become Castro's chief contribution to Marxism-Leninism. In a later speech, he spoke at great length in this vein. He told how the Schools of Revolutionary Instruction were really schools of Marxism-Leninism, how the *Granjas del Pueblo* were really *sovkhozes*, and how the peasants' fear of "cooperatives" had inspired him to organize them into something new to be called *Sociedades Agrícolas*, or Agricultural Societies (*Revolución*, December 22, 1961). And in his interview on January 23, 1962, with the editor of *Izvestia*, A. I. Adzhubei, and the editor of *Pravda*, P. A. Satyukov, Castro admitted that "the agricultural cooperatives are in their character very close to the *Granjas del Pueblo*" and that the new *Sociedades Agrícolas* would be much more like traditional cooperatives (*Revolución*, January 30, 1962). Thus, it is now official that the 1959–61 "cooperatives" were misnamed and misleading; like so much of the *Fidelismo* of that period, they served the purpose of selling one thing and calling it another, a feat of false "packaging" that might be envied on New York's Madison Avenue.

Other things became clear at the Eleventh Congress of the Cuban Confederation of Labor, toward the end of November, 1961. The congress named the veteran Communist trade-union leader Lázaro Peña as Secretary General, and thus formalized what had been a fact for many months. The Minister of Labor, Martínez Sánchez, made a startling and most indiscreet reference to the previous trade-union congress in November, 1959, at which a bitter struggle had taken place between the 26th of July adherents and the Communists, and had ended only with the intervention of Castro himself on behalf of the Communists in the name of "unity."

> Those rascals are not here who shouted "26! 26!" in order to oppose the unity of the workers' movement; and it is to the glory of the revolution and the people that there certainly are not here those rascals who ran from one side to the other while the congress was going on and shouted in the aisles, "*Melones! melones! melones!*" ["melons"]. They are not here, but the "*melones*" are here with you! The "*melones*" are here, and we will continue to be "*melones*," because we will continue being green outside and red inside! [*Revolución,* November 27, 1961].

Here, again, the novelty is not what was said but who said it. Martínez Sánchez, one of those lawyers who have been so numerous and instrumental in this "workers' and peasants' revolution" (there is still not a single worker or peasant in Castro's Cabinet), has long been considered the key man in the maneuvers that turned the Cuban labor movement over to the Communists. But those who had dared to say so had opened themselves to the charge of "anti-Communism," which, since the end of 1959, has been officially equivalent to "counterrevolution." Now the counterrevolutionary truth has become the revolutionary truth. Martínez Sánchez has been one of the leading men of Cuba's government since January, 1959, when he was appointed Minister of Defense, and his self-portrait as a *melón* makes one further wonder about Professor Mills's classification of Communists and "Communist-types." In what category do the *melones* belong?

The two official Communist spokesmen at the trade-union congress, Lázaro Peña and Blas Roca, also made revealing contributions. The former did so by employing a rather new formula: "The Revolutionary Government, directed today by the ORI, tomorrow by the United Party of the Socialist Revolution" (*Revolución*, November 27, 1961). Though his speech did not lack the usual obeisance to "*nuestro héroe y líder máximo*," Fidel, the hegemony of the party had never before been stated quite so pointedly. Blas Roca left no doubt, however, where Fidel fitted into the scheme. By chance, Roca was introduced as Secretary General of the ORI, and he carefully disclaimed that role, which, he said, belonged to Fidel Castro. Then he declared: "Fidel is not only the *Líder Máximo* of the revolution, he is not only our national hero. He is also the *Líder Máximo* of the Cuban working class; he is also the best fighter that we have in Cuba for socialism" (*Revolución*, November 28, 1961).

Thus, a *quid pro quo* had clearly been worked out. The Communists agreed to recognize Castro as the leader of the new party; Castro agreed to recognize the party as the leader of the revolution; and the party could be recognized by its "Marxist-Leninist" principles and "democratic centralist" organization.

As the trade-union congress ended, "revolutionary terror" was officially introduced in Cuba. It took the form of Law No. 988, dated November 29, 1961, providing the death penalty for all those who take up arms against Castro's regime or even burn sugar cane (a tactic once used by Castro). The occasion for this law was the reported murder of a sixteen-year-old member of a "literacy brigade" and a peasant by unidentified assailants two days earlier. The law was so drastic and received so much publicity, including a major speech by Castro himself, that its roots were obviously deeper. In fact, Castro had said that the revolutionaries would have to "annihilate" the counterrevolutionaries or vice versa as early as January, 1961, even before the attempted invasion (*Obra Revolucionaria*, January 4, 1961). At that time, a law was passed condemning "terrorists and saboteurs" to sentences of from twenty years' imprisonment to death. In his speech on the new law, however, Castro for the first time used the phrase "revolutionary terror"; he served notice that the accused could expect only "a simple and rapid procedure" and execution of the sentence in forty-eight hours (*Revolución*, November 30, 1961).

For over a year, however, political prisoners have not received any trials at all, and the case of David Salvador, the former leader of the anti-Batista trade-union underground and head of the Confederation of Labor in the first year of Castro's regime, is one of those scandals which, if it took place in Franco's Spain, would inspire petitions of indignation and appeals for mercy from radicals and liberals all over the world. There is, clearly, one justice for totalitarians of the Right and another for totalitarians of the Left. If Batista, whose regime was brutal enough, had dealt with Castro—who had after all directed an assault on an army barracks—and other 26th of July leaders in the same manner Castro now proposes to deal with his opponents, there would be no Fidel Castro, no Armando Hart, no Osvaldo Dorticós to inaugurate a state of "revolutionary terror."

Cuba has, then, entered into a stage of forced industrialization, revolutionary terror, and a totalitarian state party. It is no accident, I feel, that they have all come together at the same time. The Castro regime has embarked on a policy which in the end cannot be prosecuted without a growing terror and a totalitarian machine. There is, of course, a fatal logic in the course that Castro is now pursuing—in his own words, "*lucha a muerte*" ("war to the death"), a struggle of "extermination." Those who aim at total power must "annihilate or be annihilated," but it was precisely this deadly game that this Cuban revolution once proudly boasted it would refuse to play, and I hardly believe that it would have seemed so appealing to so many people if they could have foreseen that it, too, would end in terror and totalitarianism.

THE BALANCING ACT

In substance, there was very little for Castro to say in his much-heralded and almost as much misinterpreted speech of December 1, 1961.* In most of the speech, he merely played variations on themes that had appeared in many of his statements during the past year. Unfortunately, the first reports of the speech were misleading; they were based on mangled phrases, taken out of context, that gave the impression that he had always been a Communist and had perpetrated a historic fraud. The main purport of the speech was, if anything, quite different.

On December 1, Castro was again faced with the delicate task of explaining how and when he had become

* Castro's speech was handled in Cuba in a way that created much confusion in the United States and perhaps elsewhere. He began speaking at about midnight and finished at 5:00 A.M. Though he spoke on December 2, the official date for it in Cuba is apparently December 1, and I have decided to follow this usage in order to avoid even more confusion. The first edition of *Revolución* of December 2, 1961, carried a preliminary "free version" of the first portion of the speech only; a second edition that same day carried the speech in full. Eleven and a half pages of the speech appeared in the weekly magazine *Bohemia,* dated December 10, 1961. A comparison of this version with the full text shows that *Bohemia* published only about 40 per cent of the total, without in any way indicating that it was only a partial version. The full text also appeared in *El Mundo* and *Noticias de Hoy* of December 2, 1961. The failure of *Revolución* to carry the full text in its first edition, which was the only one to arrive in the United States at the time, and the abbreviated version in *Bohemia* gave rise to rumors and interpretations for which there was no foundation.

a Communist. In the past, as I have noted, he had always blamed himself for having been so ignorant and naïve. This again was his main motif, but it was not the only one.

He called himself a "political illiterate" until his graduation from high school–not until, as his words have been misconstrued, his graduation from the university.* Why had he been so blind? His "class origins," he said, were to blame. But others–he dwelt at length on Marx, Engels, and Lenin–had overcome this handicap, and so, he implied, had he.

In another section of this speech, he clearly intimated that he had taken the first steps on the long road to "Marxism-Leninism" in the university:

> I always remember that, during my first contacts in the university, I began to enter into disagreements and to conceive some revolutionary ideas while studying bourgeois political economy. Later, naturally, we began in the university to make the first contacts with the *Communist Manifesto*, with the works of Marx, Engels, and Lenin. That marked a process. I can say, as an honest confession, that many of the things that we have done in the revolution are not things that we invented, not in the least. When we left the university, in my particular case, I was really greatly influenced– not that I will say I was in the least a Marxist-Leninist. It is possible that I may have had 2 million petty-bourgeois prejudices and a series of ideas, nevertheless, that I am very glad I do not hold today, but fundamentally . . . And probably if I had not had all those

* Castro used the expression "*bachiller*," which, in Cuban usage, refers to graduation from the equivalent of high school–not, as in the term "bachelor of arts," graduation from college.

> prejudices, I would not have been in a position to make a contribution to the revolution such as we did make.

Castro was torn in this speech between the desire to repudiate his past in order to get closer to the Communists, and the desire to salvage his past in order to preserve his revolutionary leadership. His speech was a balancing act, leaning sometimes to one side, sometimes to the other. Whenever he went too far in one direction, he seemed to catch himself and start off in the other direction, as in this reminiscence of his trial in 1953:

> I recall that on that occasion some books that we carried with us, including one by Lenin, were taken by the police. And then, one of the lawyers at the Moncada trial asked: "And that book? Whose was it?" "That book was ours." And, to be sure, since I was a little irritated, I went on and said: "Yes, that was our book, and anyone who does not read those books is an ignoramus," and that was that!
>
> Then, already by that time, our revolutionary thinking was, on general lines, formed. Nevertheless, we were not complete revolutionaries; we were much more revolutionary when we came to power. We are [now] convinced revolutionaries.

Paragraph after paragraph wavered between self-congratulation and self-disparagement:

> I consider myself more revolutionary than I was the first of January [1959]. Was I a revolutionary on the first of January? Yes, I believe that I was a revolutionary on the first of January. That is to say, all the ideas I have today I had the first of January.
>
> Well then, am I at this moment a man who has

> studied completely the whole political philosophy, the whole history, of the revolution? No, I have not studied it completely. Of course, I am absolutely convinced and I have the intention—which is the intention all of us should have—of studying.

In a curious catechism, he managed to believe in Marxism in 1953, in 1959, and today, without having quite understood it:

> Do I believe absolutely in Marxism? I believe absolutely in Marxism! Did I believe in it on the first of January? I believed on the first of January! Did I believe on the 26th of July [1953]? I believed on the 26th of July! Did I understand it as I understand it today, after almost ten years of struggle? No, I did not understand it as I understand it today. Comparing how I understood it then with how I understand it today, there is a great difference. Did I have prejudices? Yes, I had prejudices; yes, I had them on the 26th of July. Could I call myself a full-fledged revolutionary on the 26th of July? No, I could not call myself a full-fledged revolutionary. Could I call myself a full-fledged revolutionary on the first of January? I could not [even?] call myself almost a full-fledged revolutionary.*

And finally, he cried out, "I am a Marxist-Leninist, and I will be one until the last day of my life."

Yet, he came back again and again to the "prejudices" he had long had against the Communists. He spoke as much of his differences and difficulties with them as of

* It is clear that this speech gave little or no confirmation to the story of Salvador Díaz Versón that Castro had "entered the service of the Soviet Union" in 1943 at the tender age of seventeen, or that of Nathaniel Weyl that Castro had become a "trusted Soviet agent" by 1948, or that of Daniel James's informants that Castro had "received his final indoctrination in Communism" in Mexico in 1955–56.

the aims and ideas they had had in common, and everything else he said must be understood in this context. A typical passage reads:

> Did I have prejudices? I think it is good to speak of this. Did I have prejudices with respect to the Communists? Yes. Was I influenced by the propaganda of imperialism and at any time by the reaction against the Communists? Yes. What did I believe of the Communists? Did I believe that they were thieves? No, never; I always considered the Communists—in the university and everywhere—to be honorable people, honest and all that. But, good, this has no special merit because almost the whole world recognizes this. Did I have the idea that they were sectarian? Yes. Why did I have these opinions about the Communists? Simply because, I am absolutely convinced, the ideas I had about the Communists—not about Marxism, about the Communist Party—were, like the ideas of many people, a product of propaganda and the prejudices inculcated since childhood, practically, almost since school days, in the universities, everywhere, in the movies and all other places.

In other passages, however, Castro tried to extract some comfort from his past political backwardness by pointing out that his fuzziness had enabled him to appeal to many more people than the Communists could have reached. In one sentence, he observed that "if I had been in the situation of Carlos Rafael [Rodríguez], at best when we went to the mountains, we would have had a very much more difficult situation there." This point was developed in a much longer section, which has the added interest of hinting that he had not always been what he had pretended to be. He declared that his speech at the Moncada trial, the "History Will Absolve Me" speech, had been deliberately toned down in its radicalism in order to make the movement as broad as possible. This was as close as he came to implying that he had been closer to the Communists than he had admitted, but it was still far from any suggestion that he had been a "secret Communist," as some sensationalized versions of the 1961 speech claimed. Here, again, his main purpose seemed to be to claim some credit for his previous position, which had differed from the Communists but, for that reason, had been more successful in beguiling the Cuban masses. Yet the speech was full of other types of trickery; Castro repeatedly boasted how he had signed pacts he had had no intention of honoring, and how he had worked with people he had had every intention of destroying.

The last section of Castro's speech was devoted to his relationship with the new party. In the past, he conceded, he had exercised power alone; the time had come for power to be shifted to the revolutionary party. He explained his previous one-man leadership as "simply the consequence of the revolutionary process," but it was now "wrong," because only the party could guarantee "the continuity of power and of the revolutionary line." He proclaimed his faith in and subordination to the party in such professions as, "I believe that the ideal system, the most perfect found by man to govern a country," though transitory, "is the system of government on the basis of a revolutionary party, democratically organized and with a collective leadership. This means that the party should exercise the functions of leadership." The program, of course, would be "a Marxist-Leninist program adjusted to the precise objective conditions of our country."

BURY THE DEAD

Subsequent speeches by Castro went over the same ground, sometimes emphasizing one thing, sometimes another. On December 20, 1961, he made a revealing effort—as if he were troubled by a guilty conscience or knew that he had skirted too close to an admission of political fraud—to absolve himself of having perpetrated systematic deception:

> Of course, no one is being deceived, no one here has ever been deceived, we have never deceived anyone. What have we done? Well, we understand this reality, we have acted in a Marxist-Leninist manner; which is to say, we have taken into account the objective conditions. Of course, if we stopped at the Pico Turquino [a height in the Sierra Maestra] when we were very weak and said, "We are Marxist-Leninists," possibly we would not have been able to descend from the Pico Turquino to the plain.
>
> Thus we called it something else, we did not broach this subject, we raised other questions that the people understood perfectly.

If this were all he had said, it might be imagined that he had reached the stage of portraying himself as, even in the Sierra Maestra, a Marxist-Leninist who had for tactical reasons "called it something else." Incredible as it may seem, all the promises and programs between 1956 and 1958 in which he had sworn allegiance to general elections and all the freedoms guaranteed by the 1940 Constitution, the promises of the restoration of political parties, the distribution of land to the peasants instead of state farms, just compensation to expropriated owners, free trade-unionism, and all the rest—all these have been blotted out as if they had never existed. Where had they fitted into his "Marxism-Leninism"? The closest he has ever come to an explanation is in more and more frequent references to the familiar Communist doctrine of "objective conditions." When these conditions are unfavorable, Communists consider it permissible and even necessary, in Lenin's classic phrase, "to resort to all sorts of devices, manoeuvres, and illegal methods, to evasion and subterfuge."* In the name of "objective conditions," then, Communists may justify any deception, as long as it is aimed against the enemy, and even if the enemy is temporarily deceived into regarding itself as the Communists' ally. But Castro still wants to have his cake and eat it too; he indignantly denies that he ever deceived anyone about anything, and almost in the same breath justifies his deceptions on the ground of "objective conditions."

In another passage in the same speech, Castro seemed

* Lenin used these words in connection with penetrating into and carrying on Communist work in trade unions ("*Left-Wing*" *Communism: An Infantile Disorder*, New York: International Publishers, 1934, p. 38). Castro's situation in the Sierra Maestra would certainly represent an even more justifiable occasion for putting them into practice.

to shy away from the previous implication that he had been a Marxist-Leninist in the Sierra Maestra but had "called it something else":

> Were we full-fledged Marxist-Leninists? No, we were not full-fledged Marxist-Leninists. I was, for example, a type of Marxist-Leninist who had been struggling with a number of ideas that I had taken from Marxism-Leninism in my formative period—and it certainly was a formative period—a series of things which I believed in as fundamental truths, and made action conform to these fundamental truths [*Revolución*, December 22, 1960].

Here, he is only "a type of Marxist-Leninist" who had not known that he had been one, a veritable Communist Monsieur Jourdain. But in the same sentence, even this is weakened by reference to a "formative period," a formula loose and vague enough to mean anything or nothing. Many young Cubans had also had a smattering of the *Communist Manifesto* and the works of Marx, Engels, and Lenin in the university without having become Communists ten years later. Only after having become a "Marxist-Leninist" could Castro look back at his rather checkered past and call it a "formative period," as in a sense it would have been no matter what the outcome.

Still later, at a press conference on January 17, 1962, Castro spoke of himself as having been a mere neophyte who had hardly taken his first lessons:

> When we began this struggle, we already had some knowledge of and sympathy for Marxism. But we could not for this reason call ourselves Marxists, as a

student of the first lessons of music cannot call himself a teacher of music. We were revolutionary apprentices, and we learned rapidly and quickly, that is to say, rapidly and well. Which is to say, we had this vocation, we were inclined in that direction; we were acquainted with the first notes, and we received in the course of the struggle not only a theoretical education but another type of great education, which is practical education. Not only did we learn from books but we have learned from that great teacher which is the revolution itself [*Revolución*, January 18, 1962].*

It is clear from all this that these speeches cannot be understood by means of isolated snips and pieces. They were made by a man who had to reconstruct his past to fit his present in order to make himself retroactively worthy of becoming Secretary General of a "Marxist-Leninist" party. His memory of the past has become extremely selective, and whole areas have been expunged from the record. This is not a new phenomenon in Communist states; history has been rewritten innumerable times in the Soviet Union, and it is now being rewritten in Cuba, primarily by Castro himself. In a curious way, Castro and some of his most bitter enemies, who always considered him a Communist, now had a mutual interest in giving him a respectable Communist genesis. Those who would not believe a word Castro said when he denied having been a Communist were ready to believe every word he said when they thought he was admitting having been a Communist.

In effect, these speeches were Castro's ultimate effort

* Castro repeated almost the same words in his interview with Adzhubei and Satyukov (*Revolución*, January 30, 1962).

to bury his past as a *Fidelista* and to initiate his career as an avowed Communist. They raised almost as many questions as they pretended to answer because so much consisted of a play on words—"Marxism," "Marxism-Leninism," "socialism," "revolutionary," "*cabal*" ("full-fledged"). But where one begins and another ends was never made clear, and a good deal was still another semantic smoke screen. From the Communist point of view, there is only one "Marxism" today and that is "Marxism-Leninism," and there is only one "Marxism-Leninism" and that is whatever the Communists say it is. In his references to the official Communist leaders, Carlos Rafael Rodríguez, Blas Roca, and the rest, as the most *cabal* revolutionists, Castro made sufficiently clear in what context these much-abused words were supposed to be understood.

It is an almost hopeless task to sum up these speeches in a few words, but for me, there were four main elements in what he tried to say:

(1.) Practical and political differences held him apart from the official Communists at least through part of 1959. (2.) He went over to them bag and baggage as a result not only of concrete pressures after the taking of power but of latent tendencies within him that go back to his university days. (3.) He was able to win a broad base in the struggle for power precisely because he had not been a conscious Communist. (4.) He had deliberately concealed his true tendencies, deceived those who had believed in him, and betrayed what he had claimed to stand for in order to obtain a broader mass base than the Communists could obtain.

In my first article, in *Encounter* of March, 1961 ("The Two Revolutions"), I ventured to put forward a tentative theory to account for what I called the Cuban "variant" in the "Communist family of revolutions." In brief, I suggested that Fidel Castro had been "suddenly and unexpectedly catapulted into power without a real party, a real army, or a real program." He had never been identified, in the struggle for power, with any original economic or political ideas, and had differed from Batista's other enemies chiefly in his faith in armed struggle. His political gifts were of a demagogic, not a creative, order. The Communists were able to fill this vacuum in him, once they had made up their minds that they could win power, not against him, but only through him. And it was also a deep, inner inadequacy which made him incapable of turning from the original course of his revolution to any other that was truly independent and indigenous. He did not have the disciplined and experienced cadres, the ideology, and the international support to shift from one type of revolution to another, and only the Cuban and Russian Communists could make them available to him. Yet he would serve the Communists only on condition that they should appear to be serving him. And if the "united party" materializes, I wrote, "Fidel Castro will certainly go down in history not as the *Líder Máximo* of a new movement but as the Pied Piper of an old one."

Castro's self-analysis on December 1, 1961, was, in essence, not very different from this interpretation. In the main, he sought to blame his former disagreements and frictions with the Communists on his class prejudices, his lack of understanding of Marxism, his susceptibility to imperialist and reactionary propaganda, his "ingenuousness." His real conversion to Communism, he implied, had come *after* he had taken power, when he had realized that he was trying to make "a socialist revolution without socialists" and needed the "experienced cadres" of the PSP. More than once he took pains to acknowledge that the Communist old-timers—Juan Marinello, Aníbal Escalante, Blas Roca, and Carlos Rafael Rodríguez, especially the latter, who seems to have become his latest mentor—had known more about the revolution than he had known, and that he had merely become a "student" of Marxism-Leninism.* Despite the backing and filling in this speech, Castro's professions of inadequacy and inferiority rang true to me. There can no longer be any doubt that Fidel Castro has been the Pied Piper of the Communist movement rather than the *Líder Máximo* of a new one. Those who wish to dispute this must hereafter argue with Fidel himself.

CASTRO AND THE UNITED STATES

Yet how could so many be so wrong?

Jean-Paul Sartre wrote a book about Cuba in which he fleetingly mentioned the Cuban Communist Party only twice, and in reference to a period long before Castro took power. The reader is inescapably left with the impression that the Communists, in the spring of 1960, were so unimportant that there was virtually noth-

* Not yet an advanced student, as his reference to Engels, who lived on the profits of textile mills, as a "*comerciante*" ("merchant") would indicate.

ing to say about them. In September of that year, after Blas Roca's call for "fusion," Sartre wrote an introduction for the Brazilian edition of the book in which he angrily denied that there was any danger of the Cuban revolution becoming Communist or even that the Cuban Communist Party wanted it to become Communist. "No," he maintained, "if Cuba desires to separate from the Western bloc, it is not through the crazy ambition of linking itself to the Eastern bloc."

Leo Huberman and Paul M. Sweezy wrote a book on Cuba in 1960 in which they concluded that "the hypothesis of Communist infiltration of the leadership is a pure figment of the anti-Communist imagination." In the July–August, 1961, issue of their magazine, *Monthly Review*, they published an article by J. P. Morray which finally admitted that Fidel had become "a kind of Marxist-Leninist" and that party "fusion" was coming, but protested that "it is inconceivable that Fidel would accept, or that the Party would ask him to accept, subordination to its collective judgment."

I have alluded to the treatment of Cuban Communism in C. Wright Mills's book, but another passage in it is worth noting because it deals with an alleged cause of Castro's Communism:

> Our Prime Minister went to Washington, right away after the insurrection, but he was just given the cold shoulder, and certainly no help. Even his request for quite minor financial consideration was turned down flat.

The United States has surely been guilty of many selfish and stupid actions in its relations with Cuba in this century, but the incident of April, 1959, does not happen to be one of them. Castro himself went to some pains to deny any desire to negotiate on that trip, and three financial experts whom he brought with him have testified that he forbade them to ask for American aid or even to enter into economic and financial discussions in Washington. The theory that Castro wanted American aid but turned to Soviet Russia and Communism in frustration makes a very neat and simple propaganda package, but it is an unmitigated myth, unworthy of an academic moralist.

On April 17, 1959, in his speech before the American Society of Newspaper Editors in Washington, Fidel Castro declared (in English):

> I wish to explain that we did not come here for money. It is possible that many other governments have come here for money, and many people believe that every time some government comes here, it is coming for money. I was more interested in public opinion than in money. And I was not agreed that the aim of the travel be confused [*Problems of Journalism*, Proceedings of the American Society of Newspaper Editors, 1959, p. 82].

Former Finance Minister Rufo López Fresquet has stated:

> When I accompanied Fidel to this country in April, 1959, the Prime Minister warned me as we left Havana not to take up Cuban economic matters with the authorities, bankers, or investors of the North. At various times during the trip, he repeated this warning. That is why, when I visited the then Secretary of the Treasury, Robert B. Anderson, I did not respond to the

American official's indications that the United States was favorably disposed towards aiding our country. Also for this reason, during our stay in Washington, when I exchanged views with Assistant Secretary of State for Latin American Affairs Roy Rubottom, I feigned polite aloofness to his concrete statement that the U.S. Government wished to know how and in what form it could cooperate with the Cuban Government in the solution of the most pressing economic needs [*The Times of Havana* (Miami), September 15–17, 1961].

Another of the Cuban financial experts, former President of the Cuban National Bank Felipe Pazos, has told of the meeting attended by Secretary Rubottom, officers of the Department of State and Department of the Treasury, Cuban Finance Minister López Fresquet, Minister of Economy Regino Botí, and himself. The Americans, who had taken the initiative in calling the meeting, repeatedly asked the Cubans to state what the United States might do to help economically and financially. Bound by Castro's instructions, the Cubans could only answer that they needed no help and had no requests to make. Pazos went through the same experience at the International Monetary Fund. Another Cuban expert, Dr. Ernesto Betancourt, has made the same disclosures.

This does not mean that financial or economic negotiations between the United States and Cuba would necessarily have ended happily. It does mean, despite a widespread impression to the contrary, that Castro did not even wish to try. It might be argued that the revolution he had in mind could not be supported by the United States, but that is not how his propagandists have put it.

They have preferred Professor Mills's more lurid version of the "cold shoulder" for even "quite minor financial consideration."

Claude Julien is still the prisoner of this thesis, which he had expounded also in his book, *La Révolution Cubaine*. Thus, he wrote in *Le Monde* of January 3, 1962: "And each time that the tension between Washington and Havana increases, moderate elements abandon the revolution, making room for men more to the Left, including the Communists." This is simply a historical legend—to use no harsher term. The "moderates" did not "abandon" the revolution; they were forced out. In the first half of 1959, the "moderates" watched apprehensively as key positions in the army, the secret police, and elsewhere were turned over to the Communists. By the fall of 1959, when the "moderates" tried to call a halt, it was too late, and they were ruthlessly crushed as "traitors" and "counterrevolutionaries." The turning point represented by the arrest of Major Hubert Matos in October, 1959, had nothing to do with any increasing tension between Washington and Havana; it was wholly rooted in the increasing tension between the old leaders of the 26th of July Movement and the Communist PSP. The trade-union leader David Salvador was as "anti-Yankee" as any Cuban revolutionary; he was simply and solely opposed to turning over the Cuban trade-union movement to the Communists; he was eliminated for that reason and no other. Indeed, it is an arrant oversimplification to suggest that the internal struggle was between "moderates" and "radicals." Quite a few victims of the Communist takeover were anything but "moderates," especially in their attitude toward United States investments in Cuba (and Right-wing Cuban circles in the United States have not yet forgiven them). The true dividing line was between radical democrats and Communist totalitarians, and Julien has unfortunately dedicated his journalistic talents to blurring this essential reality.

In his commentaries on Castro's speech both in *Le Monde* and in *France Observateur* of January 4, 1962, Julien pursued his vendetta against the United States with the one-sidedness and persistence of an intellectual obsession. He attributed Castro's pro-Communist actions to the overt economic hostilities that broke out in the summer of 1960, whereas Castro had made his crucial decisions in favor of the Communists many months before. The fundamental weakness in Julien's analysis lies in the fact that Castro's collaboration with the Communists was sealed in 1959, when United States policy was largely based on a "wait and see" attitude, and not in 1960, when the United States decided that Castro had gone too far in his collusion with the Communists to turn back. The decision to turn Cuba into a Communist state was of such fundamental magnitude that it cannot be ascribed to a mere reactive response. A political leader who rejects Communism for the reasons that Castro had allegedly rejected it does not embrace it out of pique or even revenge—not if he wishes to be taken seriously. I do not wish to make Julien's mistake in reverse and deny the significance of U.S. policy in Cuban developments. But it was not the causative, operative factor. And Castro, in his speeches of December, 1961, and after, did not try to make the United States policy in 1960 the causative, operative factor of his conversion to "Marxism-Leninism." In effect, Castro's speech of December 1, 1961, was one long refutation of Julien's favorite thesis.

Could any other American policy have made a difference? The answer, it seems to me, depends in large part on the time factor. In the period 1953 to 1958, it might have made the greatest difference. From 1953 to the middle of 1957, the American Ambassador in Cuba was an unabashed admirer and ardent abettor of Batista. His successor was gullible enough to bank on a pledge by Batista to hold "honest elections" in 1958. High-ranking American military officials bestowed medals and honors on Batista and his leading military aides, including those with the most unsavory reputations. Members of Congress and even Vice President Nixon made extravagant statements in praise of Batista in brief visits to Havana. I am inclined to agree with Professor Frank Tannenbaum that "If we had denounced Batista for overthrowing an elected government and offered to help its reestablishment, there would in all probability never have been a Castro."*

Yet, by 1958 and even before, the pro-Batista group considered itself out of sympathy with the policy-makers in Washington, and it later charged that Washington had "pulled the rug out" from under Batista. It would appear that American policy in this period was so inept and ineffectual that it was pro-Batista to Castro

* Professor Tannenbaum's brilliant essay "The United States and Latin America," in the *Political Science Quarterly*, June, 1961, should be required reading on the subject. It is especially recommended for members of Congress.

and pro-Castro to Batista.* On the whole, however, Batista was favored as long as he was capable of benefiting from favors, and this period constitutes a sorry and sometimes shameful interlude in the history of recent Cuban–United States relations. The pro-Batista policy has been defended on the ground that Castro wanted to substitute one dictatorship for another, but this does not explain why the United States should have supported Batista before Castro became a threat or why the United States was unable to express itself in a policy which supported a democratic, progressive Cuba and not merely one dictatorship against another.

For most people in Cuba and also in the United States, the fall of Batista seemed to open the way to a new and better day in Cuban–United States relations. This hope was frustrated, in my view, because the Eisenhower Administration was not willing or able to take any real initiative beyond sending a new ambassador with a good record and good intentions, and the Castro regime was mainly concerned with maneuvering the United States into an unfavorable position. I am all the more persuaded of Castro's bad faith by the sanctimoniously trumped-up pro-Castro propaganda about the visit in April, 1959. If Castro had been so eager to get American aid instead of Russian, he would not have deliberately kept Ambassador Philip W. Bonsal waiting three months for his first interview and then have spoken to

* This duality emerges most clearly in the testimony of the two Ambassadors, Arthur Gardner and Earl E. T. Smith, in *Communist Threat to the United States Through the Caribbean.* Hearings Before the Senate Internal Security Subcommittee, 86th Cong., 2d sess., Part 9, August 27 and 30, 1960 (Washington, D.C.: Government Printing Office, 1960).

him as to a "servant," as Castro gloated in his speech of December 1, 1961. The myth that American policy in 1959 pushed Castro into the arms of Soviet Russia and the Communists makes American policy far more active and positive than it actually was. The real flaw in American policy was sterility. If it did not push Castro into the arms of the Communists, it did very little to make it harder for him to go where he wanted to go.

CASTRO AND THE INTELLECTUALS

England has contributed its share—perhaps, more—of fine specimens of pro-Castro apologetics. In the *New Statesman* of September 17, 1960, Paul Johnson accomplished the remarkable feat of making the State Department and the CIA seem, compared to him, positively inspired:

> In Washington, a fumbling and misinformed State Department—supplied with every conceivable rubbish by the Central Intelligence Agency—assumes without question that *Fidelismo* and Communism are the same thing. This is a momentous error: seen in the future perspective of the Sixties, they are natural enemies.

A leading editorial in the *New Statesman* of April 28, 1961, called the belief that Cuba is a center for Communist subversion "a wild oversimplification." Its authority was an article in the same issue by Kingsley Martin on "Castro and the Communists."

In ten pages of their issue of May–June, 1961, the Editor and Editorial Assistant of the *New Left Review*, Stuart Hall and Norm Fruchter, took me to task for, among other things, having pointed out that the *Fidelistas* and Communists were fusing. They took the position that the *Fidelistas* and Communists were merely *coexisting* "on Fidel's terms." Interested readers may find my answer* in their issue of September–October, 1961, and events since then have dealt even less kindly with their polemic.

Another member of the Editorial Board of the *New Left Review*, Norman Birnbaum, an American by birth and education who teaches sociology at Nuffield College, Oxford, has most clearly expressed where one type of pro-Castro thinking may lead. The defense of Castro's position has brought Mr. Birnbaum to the point of proposing:

> It is possible that Communist and quasi-Communist regimes will evolve in a direction ultimately more consonant with the liberal assumptions that we all possess —rather more possible, I should think, than such evolution in many if not most anti-Communist regimes as we know them.

This thought is followed by another to the effect that "what we need is a reconsideration of the utility of concepts like liberty" (*Committee of Correspondence Newsletter*, January, 1962).

I cannot take these sentiments seriously enough to discuss them at length and, in any case, I think they would take us too far afield. I cite them because Mr. Birnbaum has dared more than most Castro supporters to draw the ultimate implications of that support. He also demonstrates most starkly how pro-Castro apologetics have

* Reprinted here as Appendix One, pp. 173–84.

changed. Not so long ago, one defended Castro as an alternative to Communism and in the name of liberty. Today, one cannot defend Castro without finding a way to defend Communism or "quasi-Communism," even if it has to be done in the most unlikely fashion as the most probable means of achieving liberalism. And "liberty" has become such a drawback that one questions, not its meaning or function, but its *utility*.

This is the authentic Castro sympathizer of 1962. But Waldo Frank, whose book, *Cuba: Prophetic Island*, was published early in 1962, is something of an anachronism. Though he was admittedly subsidized by Castro's government, I doubt whether the latter can be sure that it got its money's worth. It may not be enough for Fidel to read of himself as a "genius," a "presence," and "less the politician than the poet *and the lover*." It may mean little to him at this late date that anyone should explain in his behalf that elections would be a "bothersome delay" and an opposition press a "nuisance." For this book happened to appear, at least in its American edition, after Castro had labored for hours to explain that he had become a Communist and how inevitable it had been. Not only did Waldo Frank fail to foresee the avowal of his hero, but his book is full of earnest admonitions and exhortations against it.

Frank quotes Castro's old stricture against Communism ("the Communist state by its totalitarian concept sacrifices the rights of man") as if it still represented what Castro believes or says. He confidently advises the reader that "it is dangerous nonsense to label this deep business 'Communist.'" He warns against the Communist states' "simplistic means of nationalism, regimentation, and police power." He gives assurances that "there is not the slightest evidence that Cuba's cordial relations with Russia, China, *et al.*, commit it to give up its passionate need of nationhood or to join any bloc or party line." He worries about the danger that "subtle political and cultural pressures, alien to the Hispano-American ethos, will play on Cuba; that men in touch with Russia (including, of course, the Communist party) will win undue influence in Cuba simply because the Soviets helped Cuba in its need." He counsels Cuba, in the style of Castro's own earlier period, to "transcend" both Communism and capitalism, and to recognize that "Cuba's adversary is the Communists' and businessmen's shallow sense of man—even if they help by swapping oil for sugar."

What Waldo Frank did, in effect, was to do what so many others of his persuasion have done—to see the Fidel Castro that he wanted to see. Thus, for Mr. Frank, the Cuban "cooperatives" in agriculture and industry "could well become the nuclei of a radical syndicalism developed from the tradition of anarcho-syndicalism" and "libertarianism might flourish in Cuba within a revised syndicalism." If Fidel Castro has had any "genius," it has been this gift for getting different kinds of people to serve his purposes for different and even contradictory reasons. A generous and humane visionary like Waldo Frank could look at an imminent Communist totalitarianism and see an emergent anarchosyndicalist "libertarianism."

But how could someone like Waldo Frank, with four

decades of experience in and study of Latin America behind him, be so mistaken about a Communist regime in the making? How could he be so blind, as late as the spring of 1961, when he put the finishing touches on his book, to what Castro had done and where Castro was going?*

Other American writers have been no luckier.

In the *Hispanic American Report* of August 29, 1960, Herbert L. Matthews of *The New York Times* stated:

> Paradoxical though it may seem, Americans should be praying that nothing happens to Fidel Castro. Any

* And, it may also be asked, how could he permit himself to make so many factual mistakes in so few pages?

Examples:

The suicide of Eduardo Chibás in 1951 did not disillusion Fidel Castro with "legal methods" (p. 81). After Chibás died, Castro ran for Congress on the ticket of Chibás' old party, hardly an evidence of rejection of "legal methods." The great disillusionment came the following year with Batista's coup. And even then, Castro called for struggle against Batista in the name of restoring constitutionalism.

Castro did not "appear before" any court to protest Batista's coup (p. 83). He sent two briefs, which is somewhat different.

The U.S. military mission and arms shipments did not cease in December, 1958 (p. 129). The arms embargo went into effect in March, 1958, and the military mission was ousted by Castro in January, 1959.

Che Guevara never practiced psychoanalysis in Buenos Aires (pp. 128 and 139). His medical specialty was allergies, and he practiced medicine very little if at all before he left Argentina for Venezuela, according to the interview with his mother in *Bohemia*, August 27, 1961.

Even if Castro told him personally, Frank should have known better than that "until the sugar and oil restrictions by the U.S., there had not been so much as an exchange of letters between the Cuban and Russian governments" (p. 169 n.). The sugar restrictions—the oil incident was something else, anyway—came in July, 1960. But Soviet Deputy Premier Anastas Mikoyan signed the first Soviet-Cuban trade agreement in Havana in February, 1960, four months before the oil dispute. This agreement, with all the negotiations that preceded and attended it, was surely more than the "exchange of letters" that had allegedly not yet taken place.

> hope of changing the situation for the better lies with him.

A year later, in his curiously ambivalent book *The Cuban Story*, Matthews surrendered his faith in—though not his sympathy and, in many respects, his admiration for—Castro, whom he now seems to consider the deadliest enemy the United States has ever had in Latin America. The more ardent *Fidelistas* were displeased with portions of Matthews' book, especially those in which he remarked that the Cuban revolution was "on its way to becoming a type of Communist regime" and that the so-called party merger would be "a creature of the Communist wing, not of the 26th of July Movement." These rather temperate truisms brought down on him the disapproval of reviewers who proceeded to instruct him in the right line.

In *The Nation* of November 11, 1961, Warren Miller had the effrontery to write:

> Like his newspaper, Matthews is convinced that the new single party developing in Cuba is going to be an enlarged Communist Party; and, like his paper, he gives no evidence for making such a judgment. The new party is to be a fusion of some thirty or forty groups and, at present, there would be as much validity in prophesying that it is going to be an enlarged Women's Organization of Cuba or an enlarged Federation of University Students.

And in *The Progressive* of December, 1961, Sidney Lens had the misfortune to write:

> To dismiss the Cuban Revolution or Fidel Castro as "Communist" is to miss the lesson of history. For Castro is not now, was not yesterday, and probably never can be a Communist.

This is only a small sampling of the pro-Castro anthology that could be compiled. Yet it should be clear that I am not one of those who believes that Fidel Castro can be classified once and for all. I have written: "Still, as long as the Communists need him at least as much as he needs them, further surprises cannot be ruled out; Fidel's ego may give the Communists as much trouble as it has given many others," and later, "I cannot suppress the feeling that the new self-critical Fidel is totally out of character." I have had no reason to change my mind. There is an inherent instability in Castro's make-up that makes it hazardous to predict his future career in the Communist movement. He himself intimated as much on December 1, 1961, by remarking: "In five years we may discover that we were at this time ignoramuses." But the problem has never been whether Fidel Castro has the soul and temperament of a real Bolshevik. His very instability and inadequacy have landed him in the arms of the Communists, to whom he has turned over all the levers of power in present-day Cuba. He has gone so far that, if he should break with them, he would invite civil war in his own ranks, bring on economic disaster by forfeiting Soviet support, and totally denude himself politically and morally. What he has done is far more important than what he "is," and what he is, is far more important than whatever he was.

Among the crises that Fidel Castro must be credited with, not the least acute, I believe, is the crisis of the intellectuals who have made him their latest avatar. "He likes," Waldo Frank has written, "to have intellectuals around him, but not to discuss ideas so much as to fortify the rightness of his actions with ideas." Ever since Herbert Matthews went to the Sierra Maestra in February, 1957, Castro has been toying with sympathetic intellectuals and journalists. Matthews was fooled into reporting that Castro commanded a large force which had had many fights with and had inflicted large losses on Batista's troops. In fact, Castro then had no more than eighteen men, who had carried out one hit-and-run raid against an outnumbered enemy outpost of twelve men. This first and most famous of the "eyewitness" reports from Cuba set a pattern to this day. It cannot have been merely a succession of individual aberrations, because too many have been implicated. It has been more like a mass immersion in romantic "muck," as George Orwell called it almost two decades ago.

In a curious way, the pro-Castro intellectuals have reproduced the cycle of his own 26th of July Movement. There came a time when those *Fidelistas* who had believed in his promises of a radical democratic revolution had to choose between breaking with him or following him to the bitter end blindly. After the radical democratic revolution came the undemocratic but definitely non-Communist social revolution, original, indigenous, "do-it-yourself." Not only has he betrayed the second, too, but he now gloats that he had no intention of realizing it at the very time his intellectual spokesmen were promoting it for him. He has flaunted their gullibility as he once, with much merriment, publicly boasted how he had fooled Herbert Matthews. He has driven them to the point of no return in accepting or rejecting a Communist totalitarianism; that—and not when, why, or how he became a Communist—is the crucial issue. The Castros of this world are not only difficult for intellectuals to serve; they have nothing but contempt for those intellectuals who serve them.

The future course of Castro's revolution is not likely to be any more conventional than it has been in the past. His leadership has been marked by a peculiar combination of extreme opportunism and opportunistic extremism; he has never been wedded to lost causes or to abstract ones. He is an inherently unstable but hitherto indispensable element in an inherently unstable conjunction of forces. Those who have long dismissed him as "nothing but a Communist," and those who have deceived themselves or others that he could "never be a Communist," have both oversimplified him beyond recognition. He did not come to power or to Communism by the route of any other national Communist leader, and both the Cuban and Russian Communists have no exact precedent for dealing with him. Until he goes through the usual quota of internal crises, factional struggles, changes of line, and tests of loyalty to a higher Communist power, his place in the Communist movement cannot be fixed once and for all.

APPENDIX ONE

A LETTER TO THE *NEW LEFT REVIEW*

Dear Sir:

I hope that I may be permitted to add some further "notes" to the article in your issue of May–June, 1961, "Notes on the Cuban Dilemma," by Stuart Hall and Norm Fruchter. Since much of it was devoted to my article in the March, 1961, issue of *Encounter*, I may, perhaps, contribute something to the problems you raise by criticizing your criticism.

1. One point, I think, was unworthy of your polemical zeal. In order to give the impression that my views are not really my own, arrived at quite independently of official U.S. policy, you went well beyond the bounds of simple fairness and accuracy. You wrote: "Mr. Draper's attack echoes, in more sophisticated terms, the language and ideology of the White Paper."

I completed my article in December, 1960. The issue of *Encounter* in which it appeared went to press in February, 1961. The State Department's "White Paper" on Cuba was issued on April 3, 1961. Without knowing all these details, it should have been clear to you that a magazine dated March, 1961, could not "echo" an official statement dated April, 1961.

This was, of course, a careless slip on your part. But it was neither unrevealing nor insignificant. Your article is full of subtle and not-so-subtle allusions linking me to the State Department and Mr. Kennedy, a form of political incrimination which Leon Trotsky used to call "amalgams" and which has more recently been known as "guilt by association." Evidently you thought that you needed something more concrete to pin on me and thoughtlessly overreached yourselves.

2. Another point struck me as factually unfortunate. You charge me with making Castro's 1953 speech, "History Will Absolve Me," into a "revolutionary program" and with treating it as if it had anticipated the problems and policies of 1959. I am baffled by the gap between what I wrote and what you have ascribed to me.

First, I never "made out," as you put it, that "History Will Absolve Me" was a "revolutionary program." These are your words, not mine. Second, it is false to suggest to the reader, as you do, that I based myself on nothing more than "History Will Absolve Me." In fact, I made a "brief inventory" of Castro's political and economic promises from 1953 to 1958. By citing only the 1953 speech, you distort the issue beyond recognition. The truth is, as in the case of agrarian reform, that Castro has violated promises made even on the eve of taking power (Agrarian Law No. 3, of October 10, 1958, was only remotely related to the agrarian reform enacted in May, 1959). But you are mistaken in implying that

Fidelismo never tried to anticipate its later problems and policies programmatically. As early as November, 1956, the 26th of July Movement published a lengthy and detailed "Manifesto Program" in Mexico.

With whom are you arguing that Castro did not express in 1953 what he chose to do in 1959? Not with me. We may draw different inferences from the fact, but we agree on the fact. There are those, however, who insist that everything Castro has done, in power, is consistent with "History Will Absolve Me," that it contained the essential outline of the entire *Fidelista* revolution. Who are they? The official, orthodox pro-Castro propagandists! This is the official line, expounded in innumerable articles and speeches. On this score, we are not as far apart as you imagine.

3. More strange lapses and legends:

For some reason, you attribute to me the notion that the Cuban "revolutionary movement" was "not composed of the urban prolctariat or the peasantry, but of the middle class." On the contrary, I made it abundantly clear that the movement was composed of all classes, that the "real victor in this struggle was not Castro's 'peasant army' but the entire Cuban people," that Castro won the support "of the overwhelming majority of the Cuban middle and other classes."

You also complain that "he [Draper] fails to ask who constituted the rebel army, and who kept them alive in the Sierra Maestra." Yet I wrote of Castro's force in the Sierra Maestra that "they had to win the confidence of the peasants to obtain food, to protect themselves from dictator Fulgencio Batista's spies and soldiers, to gain new recruits." And I went to some trouble to establish the size and leadership of the rebel army.

First you invent what I did not say, and then you ignore what I did say. I did not say that the Cuban revolutionary movement was "composed" of the middle class. I said that it was *led* by the middle class—a very different matter and one with which you go on to concur. As for the rebel army, I said that its "character," not its composition, was middle class because "the character of an army is established by its leadership and cadres, which remained exclusively middle class throughout, and not by its common soldiers—or every army in the world would similarly be an army of the peasantry and proletariat." In fact, Batista's army was also largely composed of, but not led by, the peasantry.

I cannot understand this systematic distortion and vulgarization, of which I have now given sufficient examples. There is plenty to argue about in the Cuban revolution, but surely we should not waste time establishing whether I "echoed" the White Paper, whether I made out "History Will Absolve Me" to be a "revolutionary program" without reference to anything to which Castro committed himself afterwards, or whether I argued that the Cuban revolutionary movement was "composed" of the middle class.

4. I must mention one more misrepresentation because it is an aspersion that I particularly resent.

You write: "The one alienable right which neither Mr. Draper nor the White Paper, in their enthusiasm for legitimate revolutions, defends, is the right of a people to reconstruct their economic system."

I am not sure what is meant by "legitimate revolutions." In any case, my classification of Castro's two revolutions has nothing to do with legitimacy or illegitimacy. I have merely pointed out that the revolution he has made is very different from the revolution he had promised to make. If I read you correctly, you do not differ with this view, but you think that I should have put the difference between promise and performance in the perspective of the "permanent" revolution, continuously in transition. For my part, the "permanent revolution" is an elusive and questionable concept, to be used only with the utmost caution and clarity of definition; every revolution is in some sense continuously in transition; the "permanence" of revolutions is at best relative; and the Cuban revolution is today hardening into a more and more formal and familiar shape.

Be that as it may, the part that I resent is your extraordinary assumption that I would not and do not defend "the right of a people to reconstruct their economic system." There is nothing in my article or in anything I have ever written to justify this bit of malice, and it is almost degrading for one to be forced to protest one's innocence against such nonsense.

In my article, I referred, among other things, to "the social development of Cuba [which] was shockingly unbalanced in favor of the cities and towns, and Castro's crusade for the peasantry has repaid the Cuban upper and middle classes for decades of indifference to the welfare of the land workers." An opponent of "the right of a people to reconstruct their economic system" would hardly have expressed himself in this way. What I cannot and do not defend is the right of a dictator, even a "popular" dictator, to impose a dictatorship on a people in the name of reconstructing their economic system. We may differ about the nature or extent of Castro's dictatorship, or whether economic systems can be "reconstructed" without dictatorship, but your manner of posing the question *for me* was utterly inexcusable.

5. I wonder why you repeatedly chose to tilt at what I allegedly think instead of what I actually wrote. For example, you state:

> If we had learned anything from the history of post-war socialism, it is certainly that the only guarantees against abuses of all kinds are genuine democratic control from below, the right to establish social priorities and to affect their execution, the final right to overthrow a tyrannical regime, in whatever name its tyrannies are perpetrated, the freedom to dissent and criticize without fear of reprisal. Where Draper is wrong is that he does not believe these to be questions relevant to a society which has transcended the forms of a liberal democracy, whereas we see them as central to the very definition of the term socialism, whatever its forms. By imprisoning his human imperatives within one set of social institutions, Draper assumes his answers before he has come to them.

I must claim to be a better authority on what I think than you are. Not only do I consider those questions to be relevant to a society which has transcended the forms of a liberal democracy, but I believe them to be crucial.

It is precisely because I consider these questions to be relevant and even crucial that I reject the "socialism" of Soviet Russia or Cuba.

When I first went to Cuba, in the spring of 1960, and wrote my impressions, in *The Reporter* of May 12, 1960, I had not yet made up my mind where Castro's Cuba was finally going. Though I came back filled with apprehensions, I tried not to foreclose the issue. That I was anything but closed-minded or "one-sided" may be gathered from the comments made on that article by well-known pro-Castro sympathizers. C. Wright Mills called it "the most careful historical account I have seen in the American press"; Huberman and Sweezy referred to it as "generally accurate and intelligent." But Castro's regime developed in exactly the direction that I had feared the most and liked the least. When you chide me for not seeing the Cuban revolution as a "process," you are very wide of the mark, but I saw it as a process heading in the direction of a Communist totalitarianism, a variant perhaps, but essentially within the "Communist family of revolutions." We may have seen different processes, but it is hardly fair to say that you have seen a process and I have not.

No, I do not conceive of history "as committed to a determinist shuttle between liberal democracy and Stalinism." I infinitely prefer liberal democracy to no democracy at all; I think that it may be possible to go from liberal democracy to social democracy but not from Communist totalitarianism. And I am tempted to say that I can reject Castro's variant of Communism precisely because I reject the determinism of your alternatives, whereas you are more vulnerable to the wiles and guiles of Castro's Communism because you reject liberal democracy with far more ardor and enthusiasm than you reject Stalinism, its progenitors, and its successors.

6. On many questions which your article raises—whether Castro was pushed into Communism by U.S. policy, and when the turning points toward Communism came—I have already expressed myself at some length in my second article, in the July, 1961, issue of *Encounter*. There is no point in repeating myself here.

But I dare say that no reader of that article could recognize me in what you have written:

> The revolution is seen from Washington and elsewhere with eyes blurred by The Grand Disillusion with human progress. This is the ideological stance of Mr. Kennedy's "new men," who were either spurred to action by the intellectuals' fascination with the mechanism of secret intelligence, or acquiesced in a massive piece of self-deception. Such, too, is the ideological stance of Mr. Draper. . . .

Nonsense, again. I am little fascinated by the mechanism of secret intelligence, and I have never acquiesced in a massive piece of self-deception. If you are referring to the recent abortive invasion, I was far more interested in the policy that led to the disaster than to the so-called failure of intelligence. As for acquiescing in that particular piece of self-deception, you could not be less clairvoyant.

7. What, in fact, is the basic difference between us? As I see it, the issue is contained in your words: "So far, the Communists and the *Fidelistas* coexist—but the basis

of that coexistence is still contained by the definition of the revolutionary leadership in action: on Fidel's terms."

For you, then, *Fidelismo* and Communism merely *coexist;* for me, they have been *fusing.* That fusion had already gone very far by the time you wrote your article; by now it is practically complete; and the final organizational stage may be reached before these words can be published.

Is there still any doubt in your own minds about this fusion? If so, what do you make of the following:

(a) On at least two occasions, in his interview in *L'Unità* on February 1, 1961, and in his speech on March 25, 1961, Fidel virtually emptied the old-style *Fidelismo* of all ideological content by extolling the superiority of Communist ideology. "Marxism-Leninism" has now become the official Cuban state ideology. It is not quite true, then, that there is "coexistence" or that it is based on Fidel's terms; Fidel himself has accepted the Communists' ideological terms.

(b) Organizational fusion has kept pace with ideological fusion—again largely on the Communists' terms, not Fidel's, or rather their terms have become indistinguishable. *Revolución* of May 24, 1961, reported local organizational fusion in Guantánamo. Both *Le Monde* and *The New York Times* have reported the creation of a new interim organization to prepare the way for full national organizational fusion. Since Fidel never permitted the 26th of July Movement to become much more than a name, any new organization will be dominated by the old PSP, the official Communist Party, especially since its ideology will be officially Communist.

(c) Even if, as Guevara has suggested, Fidel becomes Secretary General of the new "united party," the real power will undoubtedly remain with the Communist cadres who will take over under him. Fidel is hardly the type to run the Party, and his nominal leadership would only be symbolic.

I am not one of those who feel that Fidel Castro can be classified once and for all. In my first *Encounter* article I wrote: "Still, as long as the Communists need him at least as much as he needs them, further surprises cannot be ruled out; Fidel's ego may give the Communists as much trouble as it has given many others." I am still of this mind. But any struggle for hegemony between Fidel and the Party is purely conjectural; meanwhile, he has subordinated himself to it and its ideology, and he shows no signs of drawing back. If you follow the Cuban press, you must know that day by day the Castro regime becomes more and more dogmatic, and it is a painfully familiar Communist dogmatism. Outside pressure now has little to do with it; Fidel and his closest co-workers are glorying that at last they have found the right path, the "Marxist-Leninist" path.

That Cuba belongs to the "Communist family of nations" is not my invention; Fidel and his associates proclaim it openly. They have done so ever since Guevara declared in Moscow of the eighty-one-Party declaration last December: "We had no part in drawing up this declaration, but we support it wholeheartedly." (These were his exact words, as reported by the official Cuban agency, Prensa Latina, in the Communist organ

Hoy, December 11, 1960: "*Nosotros—dijo—no tuvimos arte ni parte en esa declaración, pero la apoyamos de todo corazón.*" I have gone to some trouble to establish the original report because Guevara later toned it down to refer only to the Cuban section of the declaration, and various pro-Castro writers have made an issue of the two versions. There was not a hint of any qualification in the original Prensa Latina report. In any case, Fidel Castro himself on May 1 of this year openly associated Cuba with the entire Communist bloc.)

But if you should now be willing to admit that *Fidelismo* and Communism have been fusing, not merely coexisting, would it make any difference in your attitude and analysis? Where do you go from here?

Though I do not know you personally, from your writings I think that I can assure you that there were many Stuart Halls and Norm Fruchters among the original *Fidelistas*. They too wanted to bring about a new social order, neither capitalist nor Communist, with genuine democratic control from below, the right to establish social priorities and to affect their execution, the final right to overthrow a tyrannical regime, in whatever name its tyrannies are perpetrated, the freedom to dissent and criticize without fear of reprisal. The best and bravest of them gave up their faith in Fidel Castro as the leader of such a revolution only with the greatest reluctance and inner turmoil by the end of 1959. Some were cast into prison; some went into opposition; some have been immobilized by what they consider to be the fatal choice between Fidel Castro and American imperialism. But the Cuban Halls and Fruchters have been stilled —or they have betrayed themselves and their dreams of literally yesterday.

If you were in Cuba today, you could not fight for genuine democratic control from below, for the final right to overthrow a tyrannical regime (even if it is headed by Fidel Castro), for the freedom to dissent and criticize without fear of reprisal. You would be struck down ruthlessly and branded by a totalitarian propaganda machine as traitors.

What sense does it make for you to defend your own executioners?

Sincerely,
THEODORE DRAPER

August, 1961

APPENDIX TWO

AN EXCHANGE OF LETTERS BETWEEN HERBERT L. MATTHEWS AND THEODORE DRAPER

Dear Ted:

I need hardly tell you with what interest I read your latest contribution to the Cuban story. Once again, I find myself in what you would call an "ambivalent" position because I find so much in your study to admire and agree with, and, at the same time, so much with which I disagree. Since you discussed my work, I presumed you would be interested in my ideas.

So far as the general structure of what you write is concerned, I know it's impressive, but I remain as unconvinced as I ever was that it's possible to make the kind of blueprint you draw for the Cuban revolution and for its major leaders. I still feel that you have taken a situation after the event and then found evidence to convince you that the development was inevitable, and on the part of some of the people involved, deliberately determined. You have even apparently convinced yourself that things were not so bad under the Batista dictatorship. All this, in my opinion, simply proves that you did not know Cuba and the Cubans in the sense that you did not realize how the Cubans felt. I do not think also that you realize even remotely the human and technical problems that Fidel had in carrying out his revolution.

Most of all—and I think this is one of the greatest weaknesses of your writings on Cuba—you do not know Fidel Castro and therefore ascribe to him ideas and feelings which are almost certainly incorrect. If you had known him better, or known me better, you would not have written in your very emotional ending to the article that "Matthews was tricked* into reporting that Castro commanded a large force." There was no trickery involved. When I asked Fidel how large the force was, he refused to tell me. I guessed at the time that he had about forty men and this was roughly correct because a number of the 26th of July Movement had gone up to the Sierra at the same time I was there. Fidel admitted later he only had eighteen rifles at that time. Commanders since the dawn of history have tried to make out their forces to be stronger than they are. I was fooled, and from then until the end of the insurrection, every correspondent who went to Cuba overestimated the strength of Fidel's forces. You evidently forgot, or perhaps have not read, Che Guevara's book on guerrilla warfare. Fidel could have had a larger force from the spring of 1957 onward, if he had wanted more men. You evidently are not taking into account the elaborate preparations and the number of men and women involved in the organizing of my trip to the Sierra Maestra. You also evidently do not know that at that time there was a powerful ground swell in Havana and throughout Oriente Province against Batista. The one thing I claimed credit for in connection with the Castro interview was that I realized both his qualities as a leader and the fact that there was enough popular antagonism

* In the original article, in *Encounter*, the word "tricked" was used, but in view of the subsequent exchange of letters, I have substituted "fooled" in the present volume.—T. D.

toward Batista to make Fidel Castro and his group a formidable force.

I do not believe you have at all proved your point that Fidel "deceived those who had believed in him." By this I simply mean that it is more likely that he deceived himself.

Finally, I think it is a pity that you have allowed your emotionalism about intellectuals to lead you to imply that Fidel Castro now has "nothing but contempt for me." This happens to be 100 per cent wrong. I am sure that Fidel is disturbed by the highly critical position I have taken for a long time, but he has never done or said anything that would justify what you have written. In fact, the contrary is true.

I do not want to end on such a critical note. Let me say again that I feel you are doing something of great value in your continuing study of the Cuban revolution even though I disagree with much of what you have written.

With best regards,

Sincerely yours,
HERBERT L. MATTHEWS
Editorial Board, *The New York Times*

March 5, 1962

Dear Herbert:

We seem to read each other with mutually mixed feelings. On many things, of course, we agree. Unfortunately, the disagreements happen to come at crucial points. At least it is still possible for us to discuss our differences with candor, and that in itself is no small boon. Your letter has forced me to reconsider these painful questions, and I have decided to go into them at greater length than I have ever done before, even at the risk of sending you a letter of more pages than you sent me. These are not easy problems, especially those of a personal nature, and I know of no short and easy way of handling them.

I am not sure that I can recognize myself in your second paragraph. For the second time, you accuse me of making a "blueprint," and for the second time, I must protest. I tried to make clear that I was presenting a "tentative theory" to account for Castro's peculiar development, and events since I put it forward over a year ago have not caused me to change my mind. I suspect that any explicit theory would seem like a "blueprint" to you because, as you put it in your previous letter to *Encounter*, you see only "emotionality and irrationality" in the Cuban revolution (though this is not all you see). Is there nothing in between? Even the emotional and irrational may lend themselves to rational analysis; all historic events contain much emotionality and irrationality, but they do not prevent or preclude larger forces from operating at the same time. As I think I can show, you are not in this respect altogether consistent; you have given many explanations for Castro's behavior that add up to quite a "theory." If I were to use your terms, I would say that you also have a "blueprint," but it is implicit in what you have written and, therefore, less clear to your readers and perhaps to yourself. But more of this later.

You are equally wrong in imagining that I have convinced myself of the "inevitability" of the Cuban development. On the contrary, I think that the Cuban situation was very fluid in 1959 and that Castro might have chosen a different path. On one point, however, I am willing to plead guilty. I am satisfied that "some of the people involved" were quite deliberate in their determination of events. You yourself have written that two of the three top leaders, Raúl Castro and Che Guevara, were "pro-Communist." What is so farfetched about the idea that they have acted quite "deliberately"? It is one thing to deny or doubt that everyone in this revolution has always known where he was going. But *some?*

On the next point, however, I am somewhat stunned. I cannot understand what led you to suggest that I have apparently convinced myself that "things were not so bad under the Batista dictatorship." I merely pointed out that the role of Batista in 1938–44 was not that of the Batista of 1952–58, and that Fidel, "without too much historical verisimilitude," has reviled Batista as always a bloody and hated tyrant. There can be no doubt that Batista's political career was far more varied and complex than Fidel has liked to make it; that is all I said. The imputation that I suddenly decided to whitewash Batista was quite unnecessary.

Now as to who "knows" Fidel Castro. I am baffled by the certainty of persons like yourself that they "know" Fidel. I have never claimed to know him personally. I have studied his words and actions with some care. I have arrived at my views primarily on the basis of objective evidence, accumulated at no small cost of time and effort. You met him for the first time under very special circumstances in February, 1957. As far as I can make out, you did not meet him again until January, 1959, almost two years later. Thereafter, you spoke to him a few times, always as an outsider, even if a sympathetic one. Dozens of Cubans had infinitely more extensive and more intimate knowledge of him, and most of them lack your confidence that they really "knew" him or that he ever made it possible for them to "know" him truly. There are so many people who "knew" Fidel at one time or another and disagree so violently about him that this type of personal knowledge is obviously most treacherous or at least vulnerable. I cannot understand how you can believe that you could look into his real soul and penetrate his private mind by providing him with an audience on set occasions.

Do you really believe that he told you any more than he wanted you to believe or that he thought you might want to hear? Can you truly think that he confided to you anything but what happened to suit his immediate purposes? As a journalist, you had every right to listen to him and to use the information as you saw fit. But that is very different from getting to know the "real Castro."

You are annoyed because I wrote that Castro "tricked" you into reporting that he commanded a large force in February, 1957. Have you forgotten his performance before about a thousand people at the Hotel Astor in New York City, in April, 1959, when, with much hilarity, he described how he had bluffed you into inflating the strength of his little troop of eighteen men? Many of those present cringed at his exhibition of poor taste at the expense of one who had done so much for him. Unfortunately, I understand that there is no text of his Hotel Astor speech, but it is not needed to prove that he had misled you. Your own article of February 24, 1957, contains the evidence. It states: "They have had many fights, and inflicted many losses, Señor Castro said." And: " 'We have been fighting for seventy-nine days now and are stronger than ever,' Señor Castro said." And he also said that "Batista works in columns of 200; we in groups of ten to forty, and we are winning." In your second paragraph of that article, not quoting Castro now but in your own name, you told the reader that the cream of Batista's army was "fighting a thus-far losing battle." All this was poppycock.

I strongly doubt that your articles would have had such an electrifying effect if you had not personally vouched for Castro's large and winning force. You now claim that you "guessed at the time that he had about forty men." Then why did you report at the time, without any hint of skepticism, his boast that he had "groups of ten to forty"? And you gave a different version of this matter in your book. There you state that you saw about twenty-five and knew that others nearby brought the figure up to perhaps forty, but that where you went wrong was "to think the group I saw was a part of a large force" (p. 41). Your own article, moreover, shows that Castro helped you to go wrong. In any case, it was strange reporting to bear witness to a large force which merely existed in your imagination.

After complaining about my use of the word "tricked," you go on to admit that you were "fooled." And then you observe: "Commanders since the dawn of history have tried to make out their forces to be stronger than they are." So they have. Commanders since the dawn of history have practiced deception. Would it make much difference if I had written "fooled" or "deceived" instead of "tricked"? If so, I gladly withdraw "tricked" and substitute "fooled." The essential fact remains.

Having gone this far, I am going to continue, and try to tell you what has been so disturbing about your role in this entire affair. It has been a most unusual role for a journalist. How many journalists have been able to say, as you have said, that your articles "literally altered the course of Cuban history"? Therefore, your responsibilities have been unusually great. You have represented in this case the most influential newspaper in the United States, perhaps in the world today. Your words have been often quoted: "In all my thirty-eight years on *The New York Times*, I have never seen a big story so misunderstood, so misinterpreted and so badly handled as the Cuban Revolution." I am inclined to agree with you, but I cannot exempt you from your own criticism.

I do not wish to oversimplify. You have adopted a more and more critical attitude toward Castro's regime. Why, then, is your attitude still so disturbing? It is because, at crucial points, you always manage to find ways to justify what you claim to abhor—the turning over of the Cuban revolution by Castro to the Communists.

I am going to cite two cases in point, one from your book, the other from *The New York Times* of less than a month ago.

In *The Cuban Story*, you wrote: "By the logic of the Revolution, Hubert Matos was a traitor. Those who condemned the outrageous way he was treated, had to condemn the Revolution" (p. 155).

I gasped when I read those words. In the first place, you are one of those who profess to see no or little logic in this Revolution. When I propose a theory, you cry "blueprint." What is one to call your "logic"? In the second place, your verdict is not so much logical as political. In your own words, Matos was condemned because he "had watched the growing strength of communism in the Army with alarm. He tried to argue the matter out with Fidel, but Fidel would not listen or even see him." So, in desperation, he resigned; he was arrested; he became a "traitor."

But a traitor to *what* revolution? To the humanistic, democratic, non-Communist revolution that he had fought for? Obviously not. There can be only one answer. He was a "traitor" to the Communist "Revolution." But you do not say this. You justify his condemnation, and even the condemnation of those who protested against the outrage, by equating the Communist "Revolution" with "the Revolution." All that you had written previously should have made you come to the conclusion that the traitors were those who had sold out to the Communists. But, no, you manage to turn the case upside down before you are finished, and you join in Matos' condemnation on the ground that to resist the Communists, as he did, was to betray "the Revolution." What avail all your protestations against the Communist trend of Castro's policy when you associate yourself with this kind of "logic"?

On February 17, 1962, *The New York Times* published an editorial, "Another Cuban Communist," dealing with the appointment of a top Communist, Carlos Rafael Rodríguez, as President of INRA. What did the appointment mean? Here is what the editorial said: "What he [Fidel Castro] and his original associates obviously have discovered is that they cannot make a social revolution and run a country efficiently without training and without technically expert help." Carlos Rafael, it went on, though a Communist, has the training and technical expertness. *Ergo*, he was the right man for the job. Thus, the editorial said, "the revolution's leaders found that the only trained and prepared elements were the Communists."

Really, this is too much to swallow—in February, 1962.

In your book, you used exactly the reverse "logic" to justify the substitution of Che Guevara for Felipe Pazos as President of the National Bank of Cuba, in November, 1959. Pazos was, as you wrote, "one of the most competent and internationally renowned economists in Cuba." But then you saw fit to add: "Yet, it was a logical move at that stage. Che knew nothing about banking, but Fidel needed a revolutionary, and there are no revolutionary bankers" (p. 103).

Thus, you employed one standard when Pazos was removed and another standard when Carlos Rafael Rodríguez was installed. Pazos' fate, moreover, glaringly reveals the incredible unreality of the editorial. Before and especially after Pazos, Castro and his group systematically drove out the trained technical and professional personnel with whom, for a Latin American country, Cuba was unusually endowed. Beginning in 1959, and with increasing momentum in 1960, Communists without the slightest claim to technical knowledge took over government department after department, factory after factory, position after position.

Carlos Rafael Rodríguez is the kind of Communist intellectual who has spent most of his life as a propagandist, a writer, a teacher, not as a working economist. He is no practical expert in agriculture, though he has written articles on agrarian reform, strictly according to the Party line. In your book, you refer to him as a "newspaperman." He may or may not be an improvement over Núñez Jiménez who, by the way, was supposed to be just the right man with the right background for the job of running INRA. Soviet Russia is full of Communist economists who have not solved the food problem. In any case, the food crisis in Cuba was caused by the Communists and their servitors, and yet the editorial tells us that Fidel had to fall back on a Communist because "the only trained and prepared elements were the Communists." This premise is fantastic, but it serves the purpose of justifying another step in the Communist takeover.

I cannot claim to understand you. On one page, you write that the "logic of the Cuban Revolution" was "reprehensible," and on another page you provide a rationalization for making that logic work in the interests of the Communists. You berate me for making "blueprints," and you repeatedly take refuge in a "logic" with an implicit Communist blueprint. You think that you know Fidel Castro with an intimacy that entitles you to a special status, and you were capable of saying as late as 1960 that "Americans should be praying" for Castro because "any hope of changing the situation for the better lies with him."

In your book, despite your misgivings, you acknowledge that you retain your "sympathy" and "in many respects, admiration for Fidel Castro." I suppose that you have not been able to retain this sympathy and admiration without being dragged into a logic that another part of you considers "reprehensible."

What is "knowledge" of such a man and his works? I have tried to get it by painstaking study of what he has said and what he has done. You think you have it because you have had several tête-à-têtes with him. In the end, there are objective tests for one's knowledge. It remains for others to say how we have passed them.

Sincerely yours,
THEODORE DRAPER

March 11, 1962

Dear Ted:

I was very impressed with your letter, believe it or not, and naturally fascinated by what you wrote. I am glad you feel that we can argue this matter out with complete frankness and mutual respect. Since you have taken so much trouble in replying to me, I thought you would be interested in my keeping the correspondence going once more.

My argument about "a blueprint" would apply to any such ratiocination of a volcanic historic development—for instance, the growing reliance of the Spanish Republican Government on the Communists in the civil war.

As a journalist trying to follow the Cuban revolution from day to day, I found my own position shifting as I went along. I agree I also made some mistakes as I went along, which I tried to correct—but always with reference to what the situation was at the time.

I apologize for my implication about Batista, but that was the way your article read to me. Perhaps you did not realize how what you wrote could be interpreted. Evidently I must plead guilty to the same thing in my own writings.

As for knowing Fidel, I continue to believe that this is of the first importance. Such things are relative. As I said in my book, Fidel is an enigma and always will be one. I feel I know him within such limits, because after January, 1959, I saw him at least a half dozen times and always for hours on end—once all night and once all day. I also knew people in daily contact with him. He is a very mixed-up human being with greater limitations than I thought he had at first. But to me (and to my wife, who also knows him as I do and applies a feminine psychology), he is a very different person from the one you depict.

I suppose our argument as to whether Fidel tricked or deceived is partly semantics. However, you implied that Fidel's intention was malicious; I believe it was tactical. I was annoyed at the way Fidel brought this up at the OPC luncheon, but he has a childish streak in him and evidently could not resist. What is much more important is that there really were more people up in the Sierra Maestra than Fidel said. The forty men I said I was in contact with were around where I was. As I learned later, the Negro who became Commander of Oriente Province, Calixto García, was in the Sierra at the same time I was there and he also was fighting with a group whose size I do not know. There had been skirmishes and this was not "poppycock." Moreover, you missed the importance of the resistance all through Oriente Province, including the *guajiros* in the Sierra Maestra. I will never feel that I misled anyone by saying that Batista was "fighting a losing battle." On the contrary, I think it was a rare occasion on which I correctly grasped how a situation was going to develop.

In general, you fall into the common trap of ascribing to me approval when I am merely describing. By the revolutionary standards of Fidel and his associates, Hubert Matos was a traitor. This was revolutionary logic, and it would have been "logic" for, let us say, a Jacobin in the French Revolution. This does not mean I approve of what Fidel did; on the contrary, I deplored it, and all my sympathies were with Matos. I merely felt I understood why Fidel Castro acted the way he did. It is begging the question for you to argue now that this was an apology for "the Communist Revolution." I deny that there was a Communist Revolution at that time.

In a different way you are simply making a good debating point in arguing that I was inconsistent to see the sense of putting Rafael Rodríguez at the head of INRA and putting Felipe Pazos out of the National Bank. The cases and the reasons behind Fidel's moves are not at all comparable. For instance, I argued that Fidel could trust Che to carry on the revolution. In the same way, he now feels he can trust Rodríguez. This is what I call revolutionary logic, even though I think it is too bad for Cuba. "The trained technicians and professional personnel" you mention were not "revolutionaries" by Fidel's standards. It was stupid to alienate them, as Fidel now admits, but it was not "illogical" from his point of view at the time.

I disagree with you that "the food crisis in Cuba was caused by the Communists and their servitors." It was due to incompetence and amateurishness, making a poor method that much worse.

I argued in August, 1960, that the only hope of changing the situation lay with Fidel. No doubt it will surprise you to hear that I still say the same thing, although my hopes are dim indeed. In my opinion, this is still Fidel's revolution, and despite the Communist apparatus, the revolution would collapse overnight without him. He is a prisoner of his policies, of the forces he unleashed, and of the Cold War—but do not underrate what he is capable of doing.

With best regards,

Sincerely yours,
HERBERT L. MATTHEWS
Editorial Board, *The New York Times*

March 15, 1962

Dear Herbert:

For once, I think, something has been gained by trying to argue out deep and heated differences. It would not be fair, and it is not necessary, for me to answer you again at length. I am going to limit myself, therefore, to three remarks.

Your positions on Matos and Carlos Rafael suffer, to my mind, from a basic and pervasive confusion. The root of the problem in both cases, is: To *which* revolution was Matos a "traitor" and *which* revolution is Carlos Rafael serving? There is no such thing as "*the* Revolution." There are different revolutions, and some start as one thing and end as another. If Fidel feels that he can trust Carlos Rafael, the logic of the situation is "Communist," not merely "revolutionary." By making "revolution" and "Communist" interchangeable, or at least by sliding by the fact that they are not interchangeable, you objectively provide a "revolutionary" alibi for every step in the Communist takeover.

As for the responsibility for the food crisis, the question again is: *whose* "incompetence and amateurishness"? The Communists and those who accept their leadership have held so many key positions in Cuba for so long that they cannot be absolved of the responsibility simply because another Communist has been appointed in a desperate effort to undo the damage.

Nor do I underrate Fidel. I don't think the Communists could have taken power without him. I quite agree that they would have enormous difficulties maintaining power without him. But neither can I admire him as much as you do. If he should find it necessary, for whatever reason, to part company with the Communists, what would it mean? That he had torn the country apart in behalf of them, and then could not even live with his own doing. And if he is still capable of freeing himself from them, as you seem to hint, he would need the very people like Matos and Pazos whom he has destroyed or driven out. Where would that leave your "logic of the Revolution"?

So, I gather, we are still arguing. At least, I hope, others may be a little bit the wiser for it.

With best wishes,
THEODORE DRAPER

March 15, 1962

APPENDIX THREE

L'AFFAIRE ESCALANTE

Fidel Castro has made another "sensational" and "controversial" speech. His three-and-a-half-hour television performance on March 26, 1962, in which he denounced the Cuban Communist leader Aníbal Escalante, equaled in importance the five-hour monologue on December 1, 1961, in which he celebrated his conversion to "Marxism-Leninism." Both speeches will undoubtedly represent key points of reference in Castro's political career and the evolution of his regime.

The crucial problem in Cuba has been and continues to be Castro's relations with the official Communists, formerly organized in the Partido Socialista Popular (PSP). As long as the PSP functioned in its own name, it was relatively easy to follow its leaders and policies. But, in the middle of 1961, a so-called fusion took place among the PSP; the 26th of July Movement, Castro's original organization; and the Directorio Revolucionario, primarily a student group active in the struggle against Batista. The new party resulting from this fusion was named the Organizaciones Revolucionarias Integradas (ORI). It is supposed to prepare the way for a second and higher stage to be called the Partido Unido de la Revolución Socialista (PURS).

For some time, it has been apparent that the ORI was merely the PSP writ large. On March 26, Castro fully confirmed this view, though no one else had dared to go to such extreme lengths to show what a caricature of a "new" party the ORI has been. In effect, Castro revealed that all the positions in the ORI from top to bottom and from one end of the country to the other were mechanically filled by PSP functionaries. Aníbal Escalante, who had been organizational secretary of the PSP, became organizational secretary of the ORI, and PSP secretaries in every province and municipality simply moved into similar posts in the ORI. Indeed, as Castro put it, anyone without the right party connections "did not have the slightest hope of being chosen for anything, neither to become a technician, nor to obtain a post in one of the People's Farms, the cooperatives, the municipalities, the provinces, the JUCEI [Coordination, Execution, and Inspection Board], nor the state."

Thus the "old" Communists of the PSP succeeded in entrenching themselves in the "united" party, the ORI, to such an extent that they obtained virtually a monopoly of power. Indeed, they appropriated too much power for their own good.

As a result, the "new" Communists, who came out of the 26th of July Movement or the Directorio Revolucionario, suddenly found themselves sharply reduced in status. Their power derived primarily from their positions in the government, but the government had come to be totally subordinate to the party, and the party was wholly controlled by the former cadre of the PSP. The "cell" of the party in factories and other organizations began to make the real decisions; and the administrators, many of whom had not belonged to the PSP, were stripped of the authority to which they had become accustomed. Castro told how it had become impossible even for a Cabinet minister to change an official or an adminis trator without calling the ORI for permission, and the top ministers took their orders from Escalante directly. Undersecretaries, he said, no longer discussed their problems with their ministers but with ORI officials. Not a subject, not a question, not a detail, he went on, could be taken up without going to the organizational bureau of the ORI. "It was so extreme," said Castro, "that if a cat gave birth to four kittens, it had to be taken to the office of the ORI to see how it should be resolved."

This transference of the real power to the "old" Communists resurrected some of the former antagonism between the PSP and the 26th of July Movement. Those who came from the PSP arrogated to themselves all the rights and privileges of an ordained hierarchy, including, if Castro can be believed, packing party units and handing out jobs to their relatives. The mandate of this hierarchy was derived from the official state ideology, Marxism-Leninism, in the service of which they could claim far more years than the newcomers. The credentials of those who came from the 26th of July Movement were supplied by their struggle against Batista. After all, they protested, they had done most of the fighting while the "old" Communists had still been dallying with electoral politics.

Castro cited a number of concrete cases, all of them involving more or less obscure PSPers, but the broader implications could not be lost on his listeners. There was an ORI secretary of a group of People's Farms who had spoken contemptuously of four well-known *Fidelistas*—Captain Emilio Aragonés; Guillermo García, the first *campesino* to join the rebel army; Sergio del Valle, a doctor with the rebel army in the Sierra Maestra; and Haydée Santamaría, one of the two young women who had taken part in the Moncada attack of 1953 and had played a leading role in both the Sierra Maestra and the underground resistance. This hapless secretary, Castro said scornfully, had been "under the bed" while the other four had proved themselves in battle—a colloquial image which picturesquely expressed how most *Fidelistas* had felt about most Communists.

Another culprit had dared to criticize Castro's "History Will Absolve Me" speech of 1953 as a "reactionary document," and someone else had called the Moncada affair and the *Granma* expedition (after the name of the boat in which Castro's eighty-two men had invaded Cuba from Mexico in December, 1956) an "error." Castro related how he had encountered more than 100 officers of the rebel army who had fought in the mountains, and they told him that they were not commanding troops any longer because of their "low political level." Even Camilo Cienfuegos, one of the chief heroes of the revolution, he remarked bitterly, could have been removed from his command for this reason. And he took in even more ground by charging darkly that "certain campaigns" had been waged "in a very subtle manner" against a group of "the most valuable comrades of the revolution."

The only top Cuban Communist attacked by name was Aníbal Escalante. After conceding that Escalante was "a true Communist, an honest Communist," Castro accused him of a whole catalogue of "errors" and "crimes" ranging from "sectarianism" and "dogmatism" to converting the ORI into an instrument for personal ends, into a "tyranny" ("*coyunda*"), a "strait jacket," a "yoke," a "veritable chaos and anarchy," a "counterrevolutionary abortion." Yet, though Escalante bore the brunt of his wrath, it was clear that Castro was aiming far beyond a single individual, however highly placed in the hierarchy. For one thing, Escalante had long been the No. 2 or No. 3 figure of the PSP. A former law student, he had joined the Cuban Communist Party about 1932, had spent a long apprenticeship in Soviet

Russia, had served as editor of the official Party organ *Hoy* from its inception in 1938 to April, 1959 (when he was replaced by Carlos Rafael Rodríguez), and had then assumed the post of Executive Secretary of the PSP. He has long been considered the best brain of the Party, or at least a far better one than the General Secretary, Blas Roca. The "crimes" of Escalante, a veteran of three decades in the Party, could not help but reflect on his whole training and on all those in the Party who for so many years had put their confidence in him. In the light of his past record, Escalante was hardly one to act on his own without or against the top leadership of the PSP as a whole.

In fact, Castro made abundantly clear that he was striking through Escalante at many others. He accused Escalante of creating a "system," but the entire PSP was implicated in and had benefited from the "system." Castro himself described the system as one in which "the only revolutionaries, the only comrades who could be trusted, the only ones who could get a post in a People's Farm, in a cooperative, in the state, in any place whatever, had to be an old Marxist militant." When he spoke of the local ORI secretary who had been "under the bed" during the fight against Batista, he added ominously that this had not been an isolated case, and he promised to expose and "sweep away" all the others. The only ones, he said, who could get away with any mistakes without punishment were the "old" Communists. And of those who had been harboring any idea that he wanted to create a "cult of personality" around himself, Castro declared, "it is well to remind them of certain facts, such as the fact that we waged a war, we led it, we won it."

Castro's complaints and threats struck far beyond the person of Aníbal Escalante, and indeed, he devoted only a relatively small portion of his long harangue to Escalante. The red thread through the whole speech was the clash of interest that had developed between the "old" and the "new" Communists, and though Escalante was accused of "personal ambition," he clearly could not have satisfied it without satisfying the personal and political ambitions of the PSP's cadre and membership.

The sequence of events which led to this open clash suggests that both the issues and his own role were not quite as clear and simple as Castro tried to make them.

According to Castro, the crisis of leadership in the ORI was first brought up on January 1 of this year. This would mean that the ORI had been functioning for at least six months on the basis of virtually complete PSP control. Not until March 9 was the twenty-five-member directorate of the ORI announced, a step so long delayed that it implied an internal struggle of extraordinary virulence. In this directorate, the "old" Communists were allotted about ten seats, and Castro could count on a working majority. By this time, then, the struggle had been resolved in favor of the "new" Communists, but it was not a final and crushing defeat for the "old" ones. Despite the fact that Escalante had become the storm center of the factional struggle, he was included in the directorate, as if an arrangement had been reached which did not entail his complete elimination and disgrace. In the smaller and more powerful Secretariat of the ORI, however, only one well-known PSP leader, Blas Roca, was admitted. The other members were: Fidel Castro, First Secretary; Raúl Castro, Second Secretary; Minister of Industries Che Guevara; President Osvaldo Dorticós; and Emilio Aragonés.

On March 13, however, trouble broke out anew. At a ceremony at the university in honor of José Antonio Echevarría, who had been killed in 1957 in an attempt to overthrow Batista by attacking the Presidential palace, Castro blew up. An ORI student leader who acted as master of ceremonies read aloud the "Testament" of Echevarría and chose to omit three lines expressing his religious sentiments. Since Echevarría had been the chief founder of the Directorio Revolucionario, and had never seen eye to eye with Castro or the Communists, he represented the kind of political tendency that again must be wooed by the present regime. When Castro arose to speak, he made a scandal of this seemingly minor incident of the three lines and used the occasion to deliver an improvised but violent sermon on the evils of "sectarianism." For the first time, he used the term "*coyunda*" (literally, a strap for yoking oxen) to characterize what had happened to the revolution. But he mentioned no names, and in the same speech, he gave his blessings to the change of name of the youth organization from Jóvenes Rebeldes (Young Rebels) to Jóvenes Comunistas (Young Communists).

Thus the party split, which had been temporarily papered over on March 9, was reopened, and thereafter Castro headed for a showdown. A shakeup in the government was made public on March 24, and the whole "holy mess," as Castro called it, of Escalante and the "old" Communists was aired two days later. In this "proletarian democracy," of course, Escalante was not permitted to defend himself, and he was quickly persuaded to accept a free ride to Eastern Europe—perhaps the punishment to fit the crime.

Nevertheless, it would seem that Castro took an unusually long time to make up his mind to resist the takeover of the ORI by the PSP. Indeed, his speech of March 26 contains no little evidence that he was fully aware of what had been taking place and had played some part in making it possible. In one passage, Castro admitted not only that "we fell into the PSP's 'sectarianism,'" but that "I fell into it, in part unwittingly." Soon afterward, he observed: "Of course, we all have been responsible in a greater or lesser degree." In a rather lame effort to explain why the wrong policy had been permitted to go on for so long and to create so acute a problem, Castro made the revealing admission that the errors could not be combated until "not only the leaders, but the masses themselves, became conscious" of them. Mass pressure obviously had something to do with alerting Castro and those closest to him to the fact that the situation had become explosive and needed a drastic remedy.

This pressure undoubtedly came primarily from the "new" Communists, who had lost most from the PSP's seizure of all the levers of power by means of the new party. Yet Castro himself, all through 1961, had contributed most to the political atmosphere that had made possible the seizure of power. He had repeatedly humbled himself before the PSP's old guard and had effusively acknowledged its ideological superiority. In his speech on December 1, 1961, in which he had presented himself as a "Marxist-Leninist," he had included Aníbal Escalante as one of those old Communists whose years of service entitled them to special consideration. Yet at this very time, a ground swell was building up against Escalante's party machine, and only a month later the struggle broke out openly in the top leadership.

The exceptionally lengthy gestation period of this struggle, and Castro's equivocal explanations of his responsibility for it, give reason to believe that the initial impetus for the anti-PSP rebellion did not come from him. It apparently came from his non-PSP followers, who found themselves frozen out of positions in the party and jobs in state-controlled organizations. It is most significant that Castro's speech of March 26 never refers to questions of policy; it is almost wholly concerned with control of the party and the government. Castro himself attributed the rumors that he had been replaced by Blas Roca or by Aníbal Escalante, and that Raúl Castro had been pushed aside by someone else, to the "*mandomanía*" ("power madness") and "*gobierno-manía*" ("government mania") that had flared up.

If all had been going well in Cuba for the past year, the PSP's control might well have gone unchallenged or might have been unchallengeable. But the political crisis in the party is only part of, and partially a result of, a much broader and deeper crisis of the entire regime. A "shattering disintegration" has taken place in Cuba, as the Associate Editor of the *Montreal Star*, Gerald Clark, recently wrote after a visit there. It is a disintegration, both material and moral, that has threatened the Castro regime with losing control of the masses of people. Unfortunately for the "old" Communists, they moved to the center of the stage prematurely and exposed themselves to popular discontent just as the economy began to plunge downward. By running the country itself, instead of through others, the PSP old guard set itself up as the most eligible scapegoat in the crisis of a regime which must execute a "change of line" to obtain far more maneuvering room than it has previously allowed itself.

In this dangerously deteriorating situation, the PSP has been forced to beat a painful retreat and to sacrifice one of its outstanding leaders, Aníbal Escalante. In the showdown, it had to face the reality that it could not govern Cuba by itself and that Fidel Castro is still the essential element in the ruling equation. As Castro emphasized, the final decision to jettison Escalante was made unanimously. It is to be expected that Escalante's old comrades will now drag his name in the mud and demonstrate with countless examples that he was always a corrupting influence and treacherous deviationist.

Yet, at this stage, nothing could be more illusory and costly than the idea that Castro has "broken with" the Communists, "old" or "new." Despite all the harsh things that he said about them, he went to the greatest pains on March 26 to pay homage to their past services and to ensure their continued partnership in the party and government. The problem he faced was whether the PSP should have all power, not whether it should have none. Thus, it has been necessary to work out a new equilibrium of forces, more consonant with a shift of line to put the regime on a broader mass basis and to enable it to recapture some of the glamour of the *Fidelista* period of the struggle for power.

In essence, Castro attacked some Communists, but not Communism. On the contrary, he reaffirmed in the strongest terms his belief and faith in Marxism-Leninism and in Communism, and it is precisely in this period that he has taken to using the two interchangeably. Toward the end of his speech on March 26, he declared: "Today we are not discussing the merits of Communism or anti-Communism, or ideological definitions; the revolution is absolutely defined as Marxist-Leninist, and we are making this self-criticism of our errors within the context of Marxism-Leninism. Let no one dream of anything else or entertain any illusion about this!"

In this way, Castro served notice that Soviet Russia had little to worry about in terms of the fundamental character and future course of his regime. It is still a Communist regime, but it is Communist with a difference. Whereas previously, the old-time Communists, headed by Blas Roca and Aníbal Escalante, were the authorized interpreters of "Marxism-Leninism," now they have been succeeded by Fidel Castro. He has stepped forward, as a result of Escalante's downfall, as the final authority on "sectarianism," "dialectics," "dogmatism," "cult of personality," "revisionism," the relations between party and government, "self-criticism," texts from Lenin, and all the rest. Henceforth, Communism in Cuba will be what he says it is.

The interpretation of Cuban events has long suffered from a tendency of outside observers to go from one extreme to another. After the December 1, 1961, speech, some seized on isolated phrases taken out of context to justify what they had always thought—that Castro was and had long been a tried and true "Marxist-Leninist" or Communist. Four months later, the word may spread that he has "broken with the Communists" and was never really one of them "at heart."

In fact, as I wrote over a year ago, Castro represents a Cuban "variant" in the "Communist family of revolutions." Those who take him out of that family misconstrue his fundamental position, on which he himself insists, and those who make him identical with every other member of that family miscalculate the novelties and complexities of his position. Even though he virtually handed over the day-by-day task of running the country to the "old" Communists, forces beyond his control made it impossible for him to pursue an "orthodox" line with the official guardians of Communist orthodoxy. Castro and the Communists have driven Cuba into an impasse from which they can extricate themselves only by adopting a line of temporary concessions and compromises, of sweet reasonableness instead of extreme rigidity, of maximum maneuverability, even in relations with the United States. It is no accident that, in his speech on the Echevarría incident on March 13, Castro chose to cite Lenin's "*Left-Wing*" *Communism: An Infantile Disorder*, the classic Communist text whenever a "turn to the right" is to be executed and justified. In a larger sense, *l'affaire* Escalante was only part of a much broader maneuver that Castro's regime is now attempting to carry out.

(*The New Leader*, April 16, 1962)